Amid the Roar

A Towson University Alumni Anthology

Patapsco Valley Press

TOWSON, MARYLAND

Patapsco Valley Press
8000 York Road
Towson, MD 21252
https://www.facebook.com/PatapscoValleyPress

Publisher's Note: This book contains fictional works. Names, characters, places, and incidents of those works are a product of the author's imagination. Locales and public names are sometimes used for atmospheric purposes. Any resemblance to actual people, living or dead, or to businesses, companies, events, institutions, or locales is completely coincidental.

Book Layout © 2014 BookDesignTemplates.com

Cover art by Robert Ouellette

See page 193 for text permissions.

Amid the Roar: A Towson University Alumni Anthology—1st ed.
ISBN 978-0-9857073-0-9

For President Emerita Maravene S. Loeschke, Ph.D.

Acknowledgements

Many people helped turn this book into a reality, some by suggesting alumni authors and poets for our editors to contact, others by graciously cooperating with enthusiastic student editors for no remuneration except sharing the love of writing. Everyone who agreed to help, from administrators to authors to publishers, had the same conviction that this book would be a fitting tribute to the programs, teachers, and classmates who have made Towson a place of good education for good writers. We thank the authors collected herein for their inspiration, and we hope many more Towson students follow in their footsteps in the next 150 years. Particular thanks go to Katie Cox and Miles McQuerry as acquisition editors; Karen Saffran for many alternate cover designs; David Heckman for writing publicity copy; Katelyn Egloff and Aviva Hauser for collecting it all into the form you see here; Justin Dashiell and Mark Talbert for support with the layout; Tyler New for social networking and the problematic job of celebrity editing; Karin Yearwood for her P.R. work on Facebook; Emily Welsch for tweets and party prep; and Chris Brocato and Sarah Wilson for support with the release party. Each of these editors extended professional and collegial friendliness to the authors with whom they worked. May we see you all in the pages of the next Towson alumni anthology.

A Dream Within a Dream

Take this kiss upon the brow!
And, in parting from you now,
Thus much let me avow —
You are not wrong, who deem
That my days have been a dream;
Yet if hope has flown away
In a night, or in a day,
In a vision, or in none,
Is it therefore the less gone?
All that we see or seem
Is but a dream within a dream.

I stand amid the roar
Of a surf-tormented shore,
And I hold within my hand
Grains of the golden sand —
How few! yet how they creep
Through my fingers to the deep,
While I weep — while I weep!
O God! Can I not grasp
Them with a tighter clasp?
O God! can I not save
One from the pitiless wave?
Is all that we see or seem
But a dream within a dream?

—EDGAR ALLAN POE

CONTENTS

FOREWORD

What's permanent about a campus, itself a text to be read? Traditionally, the chapel crowned the highest hill, giving God his due; the library stood at the center, figuring a college as a bibliocentric universe; and quadrangles with lamp-lighted windows suggested at a laughable least a quiet state of study by contemporary clerks of Oxenford.

But beyond these—and the clock tower on an Elizabethan-styled building, and a later administration building styled as an Omaha Beach pillbox, and later still as a corporate box enclosing cubicles, break rooms, and windows admitting light without air, what else is lasting about a college? Surely there are students and professors, but most with a fleeting presence, and that only in alumni memories and myths.

It's the books that endure, from Aristotle on, and the scholarship and literature that professors, even long after leaving, leave. The texts that follow in this book—poems, fiction, and non-fiction—are the buildings of former students, now well-published alumni, whose work comes home to a permanent place on the Towson University campus.

What more lasting a gift by the writers to celebrate the university's 150th anniversary? And what better a wrapping than this book, completed by Patapsco Valley Press, the creation of Lana Portolano and graduate students in Towson's Master's in Professional Writing Program? Years before, professors of these author-alumni in the English department gave them pencil, eye and ear—read aloud passages even of the prose to hear rhythms Tennysonian, Plathian, and even

Popeian, all in eloquent concert. Fixtures of the department's creative writing faculty, present and past, will beam as forecasters of success: Geoff Becker, Carl Behm, David Bergman, Michael Downs, George Friedman, John Gissendanner, Clarinda Harriss, Leslie Harrison, Dan Jones, and Harvey Lillywhite, teachers good and true.

Of course, every professor in the department is a writing coach, whether of the marathon of the research paper or the sprint of the blog. For the better student writers, *Grub Street* is the English department's in-house magazine for poetry and fiction, while *Discourse* is the journal for the best student literary research and scholarship, both peer-reviewed publications promising good writing and celebrity for the student authors in the next century and a half. And the distinguished published scholarship of the faculty certifies their teaching of writing from experience.

I have a theory about their good teaching, but better things to read follow. Besides, I hear that eminent Baltimorean, H. L. Mencken, growling to keep it to myself: "Every professor must have a theory as every dog must have fleas." So read on to enjoy the best part of another Menckenian truth, "The style remains the man. What is in the head infallibly oozes out of the nub of the pen. If it is sparkling Burgundy the writing is full of life and charm. If it is mush the writing is mush too."

Cheers.
H. George Hahn
Chair
Department of English

FICTION

THE RIVER OF DANCING GODS

Jack L. Chalker *was born in Baltimore, Maryland, on December 17, 1944. He received a B.A. degree in English from Towson University and a graduate degree in English and history from Johns Hopkins University. Before becoming a full-time writer in 1978, he taught history and geography in the Baltimore City public school system. He founded a publishing house, The Mirage Press, Ltd., which produces nonfiction and bibliographic works on science fiction and fantasy. He was the author of several science fiction series including the* Well World *series, the* Dancing Gods *series, and the* G.O.D. Inc. *series. He received numerous honors including the Dedalus Award in 1983, the Gold Medal of the West Coast Review of Books award in 1984, the Skylark Award in 1980, and the Hamilton-Brackett Memorial Award in 1979. Chalker died of kidney failure and sepsis on February 11, 2005. What follows is the first chapter, entitled* Encounter on a Lonely Road, *from his book,* The River of Dancing Gods.

People taken from other universes should always be near death.
—*The Book of Rules, XX, 109, 234(a)*

Just because your whole life is going to hell doesn't mean you have to walk there.

She was walking down a lonely stretch of west Texas freeway in the still dark of the early morning, an area where nobody walked and where there was no place to walk to, anyway. She might have been hitching, or not, but a total lack of traffic gave her very little choice there. So she was just walking, clutching a small overnight bag and a purse that was almost the same size, holding on to them as if they were the only two real things in her life, they and the dark and that endless stretch of west Texas freeway.

Whatever traffic there was seemed to be heading the other way—an occasional car, or pickup, or eighteen-wheeler with someplace to go and some reason to go there, all heading in the direction she was walking from, and where, she knew too well, there was nothing much at all for anybody. But if their destinations were wrong, their sense of purpose separated the night travelers from the woman on the road; people who had someplace to go and something to do belonged to a different world than she did.

She had started out hitching, all right. She'd made it to the truck stop at Ozona, that huge, garish, ultramodern, and plastic heaven in the middle of nowhere that served up anything and everything twenty-four hours a day for those stuck out here, going between here and there. After a time, she'd gotten another ride, this one only twenty miles west and at a cost she was not willing to pay. And so here she was, stuck out in the middle of nowhere, going nowhere fast. Walk, walk, walk to nowhere, from nowhere in particular, because nowhere was all the where she had to go.

Headlights approached from far off; but even if they had held any interest for her, they were still too far away to be more than abstract, jerky round dots in the distance, a distance that the west Texas desert made even more deceptive. How far off was the oncoming driver? Ten miles? More? Did it matter?

It was at least ten, maybe fifteen minutes before the vehicle grew close enough for the woman to hear the roar of the big diesel and realize that this was, in fact, one of those haunters of the desert dark, a monster tractor-trailer truck with a load of furniture for Houston or beef for New Orleans or, perhaps, California oranges for the Nashville markets. Although it had been approaching her from the west for some time, its sudden close-up reality was startling against the total stillness of the night, a looming monster that quickly illuminated the night and its empty, vacant walker, then was just as suddenly gone, a mass of diminishing red lights in the distance behind her. But in the few seconds that those gaping headlights had shone on the scene, they had illuminated her form against that desperate dark, illuminated her and, in the cab behind those lights, gave her notice and recognition.

She paid this truck no more attention than any of the others and just kept walking onward into the unseen distance.

The driver had been going much too fast for a practical stop, a pace that would have upset the highway patrol but was required to make his employer's deadline. Besides, he was on the wrong side of the median to be of any practical help himself—but there were other ways, ways that didn't even involve slowing down.

"Break one-nine, break, break. How 'bout a westbound? Anybody in this here Lone Star truckin' west on this one dark night?" His accent was Texarkana, but he could have been from Maine or Miami or San Francisco or Minneapolis just as well. Something in the CB radio seemed automatically to add the standard accent, even in Brooklyn.

"You got a westbound. Go," came a reply, only very slightly different in sound or tone from the caller's.

"What's your twenty?" Eastbound asked.

"Three-thirty was the last I saw," Westbound responded. "Clean and green back to the truck-'em-up. Even the bears go to sleep this time o' night in these parts."

Eastbound chuckled. "Yeah, you got that right. I got to keep pushin' it, though. They want me in Shreveport by tonight."

"Shreveport! You got some haul yet!"

"Yeah, but that's home sweet home, baby. Get in, get it off, stick this thing in the junkyard, and I'm in bed with the old lady. I'll make it."

"All I got is El Paso by ten."

"Aw, shit, you'll make that easy. Say—caught something your side in my lights about three-two-seven or so you might check it out. Looked like a beaver just walkin' by the side of the road. Maybe a breakdown, though I ain't seen no cars on your side and I'm just on you now. Probably nothin', but you might want to check her out just in case. Ain't nobody lives within miles o' here, I don't think."

"I'll back off a little and see if I can eyeball her," Westbound assured him. "Won't hurt much. That your Kenworth just passed me?"

"Yeah. Who else? All best to ya, and check on that little gal. Don't wanna hear she got found dead by the side of the road or something. Spoil my whole day."

"That's a four," Westbound came back with a slight chuckle.

"Keep safe, keep well, that's the Red Rooster sayin' that, eastbound and down."

"Y'all have a safe one. This is the Nighthawk westbound and backin' down."

Nighthawk put his mike into its little holder and backed down to fifty. He wasn't in any hurry, and he wouldn't lose much, even if this was nothing at all, not on this flat stretch.

The woman was beginning to falter, occasionally stumbling in the scrub brush by the side of the road. She was starting to think again, and that wasn't what she wanted at all. Finally she stopped, knowing it was beyond her to take too many more steps, and looked around. It was incredible how dark the desert could be at night, even with more stars than city folk had ever seen beaming down from overhead. No matter what, she knew she had to get some rest. Maybe just lie down over there in the scrub—get stung by a tarantula or a scorpion or whatever else lived around here. Snake, maybe. She considered the idea and was somewhat surprised that she cared about that. Nice and quick, maybe—but painfully bitten or poisoned to death by inches? That seemed particularly ugly. With everything else so messed up, at least her exit ought to be clean, neat, and as comfortable as these things could be. *One* thing in her life should go right, damn it. And for the first time since she'd jumped out of the car, she began to consider living again—at least a little bit longer, at least until sunrise. She stopped and looked up and down the highway for any sign of lights, wondering what she'd do if she saw any. It would just as likely be another Cal Hurder as anybody useful, particularly at this ungodly hour in a place like this.

Lights approaching from the east told her a decision was near, and soon. But she made no decision until the lights were actually on her, and when she did, it was on impulse, without any thought applied to it. She turned, put down her bags, and stuck out her thumb.

Even with that and on the lookout for her, he almost missed her. Spotting her, he hit the brakes and started gearing to a stop by the side of the road, getting things stopped fully a hundred yards west of her. Knowing this, he put the truck in reverse and slowly backed up, eyeing the shoulder carefully with his right mirror. After all this, he didn't want to be the one to run her down.

Finally he saw her, or thought he did, just standing there, looking at the huge monster approaching, doing nothing else at all. For her part, she was unsure of just what to do next. That huge rig was really intimidating, and so she just stood there, trembling slightly.

Nighthawk frowned, realized she wasn't coming up to the door, and decided to put on his flashers and go to her. He was not without his own suspicions; hijackers would use such bait and such a setting—although he could hardly imagine somebody hijacking forty thousand pounds of soap flakes. Still, you never knew—and there was always his own money and cards and the truck itself to steal. He took out his small pistol and slipped it into his pocket, then slid over, opened the passenger door, and got out warily.

He was a big man, somewhat intimidating-looking himself, perhaps six-three, two hundred and twenty-five pounds of mostly muscle, wearing faded jeans, boots, and a checkered flannel shirt. His age was hard to measure, but he was at least in his forties with a face maybe ten years older and with very long, graying hair. He was dark, too—she took him at first for a black man—but there was something not quite of any race and yet of all of them in his face and features. He was used to the look she was giving him and past minding.

"M'am?" he called to her in a calm yet wary baritone. "Don't worry—I don't bite. A trucker going the other way spotted you and asked me to see if you was all right."

Oh, what the hell, she decided, resigning herself. *I can always jump out again.* "I need a ride," she said simply. "I'm kind of stuck here."

He walked over to her, seeing her tenseness and pretty much ignoring it. He picked up her bag, letting her get her purse, and went back to the truck. "Come on. I'll take you for a while if you're going west."

She hesitated for a moment more, then followed him and permitted him to assist her up into the cab. He slammed her door, walked around the truck, got in on the driver's side, released the brakes, and put the truck in gear. "How far you going?" he asked her.

She sat almost pressed against the passenger door, trying to look as if she weren't doing it. For all he knew, she *didn't* realize she was doing it.

She sighed. "Any place, I guess. How far you going?"

"El Paso. But I can get you to a phone in Fort Stockton if that's what you need."

She shook her head slowly. "No, nobody to call. El Paso's fine, if it's okay with you. I don't have enough money for a motel or anything."

Up to speed and cruising now, he glanced sideways over at her. At one time she'd been a pretty attractive woman, he decided. It was all still there, but something had happened to it, put a dull, dirty coating over it. Medium height—five-four or -five, maybe—with short, greasy-looking brown hair with traces of gray. Thirties, probably. Thin and slightly built, she had that hollow, empty look, like somebody who'd been on the booze pretty long and pretty hard.

"None of my business, but how'd you get stuck out here in the middle of nowhere at three in the morning?" he asked casually.

She gave a little sigh and looked out the window for a moment at the black nothingness. Finally she said, "If you really want to know, I jumped out of a car."

"Huh?"

"I got a ride with a salesman—at least he said he was a salesman—back at Ozona. We got fifteen, twenty miles down the road and he pulled over. You can guess the rest."

He nodded.

"I grabbed the bags and ran. He turned out to be a little scared of the dark, I guess. Just stood there yelling for me, then threatened to drive off if I didn't come back. I didn't— and he did."

He lighted a cigarette, inhaled deeply, and expelled the smoke with an accompanying sigh. "Yeah, I guess I get the picture."

"You—you're an Indian, aren't you?"

He laughed. "Good change of subject. Well, sort of. My mom was a full-blooded Seminole, my dad was Puerto Rican, which is a little bit of everything."

"You're from Florida? You don't sound like a southerner."

Again he chuckled. "Oh, I'm from the south, all right. South of Philadelphia, anyway. Long story. Right now what home I have is in a trailer park in a little town south of Baltimore. No Indians or Puerto Ricans around, so they just think of me as something a little bit exotic, I guess."

"You're a long way from home," she noted.

He nodded. "More or less. Don't matter much, though. I'm on the road so much the only place I really feel at home is in this truck. I own it and I run it, and it's mine as long as I keep up the payments. They had to let me keep the truck, otherwise they couldn't get no alimony. What about you? That pretty voice sounds pure Texas to me."

She nodded idly, still staring distantly into the nothingness. "Yeah. San Antone, that's me."

"Air Force brat?" He was nervous at pushing her too much, maybe upsetting or alienating her—she was on a thin edge, that was for sure—but he just had the feeling she wanted to talk to somebody.

She did, a little surprised at that herself. "Sort of. Daddy was a flier. Jet pilot."

"What happened to him?" He guessed by her tone that something had happened.

"Killed in his plane, in the finest traditions of the Air Force. Sucked a bird into his jets while coming in for a landing and that was it, or so I'm told. I was much too young, really, to remember him any more than as a vague presence.

And the pictures, of course. Momma kept all the pictures. The benefits, though, they weren't all that much. He was only a captain, after all, and a new one at that. So Momma worked like hell at all sorts of jobs to bring me up right. She was solid Oklahoma—high school, no marketable skills, that sort of thing. Supermarket checker was about the highest she got— pretty good, really, when you see the benefits they get at the union stores. She did really well, when you think about it— except it was all for me. She didn't have much else to live for. Wanted me to go to college—she'd wanted to go, but never did. Well, she and the VA and a bunch of college loans got me there, all right, and got me through, for all the good it did. Ten days after I graduated with a useless degree in English Lit, she dropped dead from a heart attack. I had to sell the trailer we lived in all those years just to make sure she was buried right. After paying out all the stuff she owed, I had eight hundred dollars, eight pairs of well-worn jeans, a massive collection of T-shirts, and little else."

He sighed. "Yeah, that's rough. I always wanted to go to college, you know, but I never had the money until I didn't have the time. I read a lot, though. It don't pay to get hooked on TV when you're on the road so much."

She chuckled dryly. "College is all well and good and some of it's interesting, but if your degree's not in business, law, medicine, or engineering, the paper's only good for about thirty-eight hundred—that's what I still owe on those loans, and it'll be a cold day in hell before they see a penny. They track you down all over, too—use collection agents. So you can't get credit, can't get a loan, none of that. I got one job teaching junior high English for a year—but they cut back and laid me off. Only time I ever really enjoyed life."

"So you been goin' around from job to job ever since?"

"For a while. But a couple years of working hamburger joints and all those other minimum-wage, minimum-life jobs gets to you. I finally sat down one day and decided it was fate, or destiny, or something. I was getting older, and all I could see was myself years later, sitting in a rented slum shared with a couple of other folks just like me, getting quickies from the night manager. So I figured I would find a man, marry him, and let *him* pay my bills while I got into the cooking and baby business."

"Well, it's a job like any other, and has a pretty long history," he noted. "Somebody's got to do it—otherwise the government will do *that,* too."

She managed a wan smile at the remark. "Yeah, well, that's what I told myself, but there are many ways to go about it. You can meet a guy, date, fall in love, really commit yourself—both of you. That might work. But just go out in desperation and marry the first guy who comes along who'll have you—that's disaster."

"Works the other way, too, honey," he responded. "That's why I'm paying five hundred a month in rehabilitation money—that's what they call alimony these days in liberal states that abolished alimony—and child support. And she's living with another guy who owns an auto-repair shop and is doing pretty well; she has a kid by him, too. But so long as she don't marry him, I'm stuck."

"You have a kid?"

He nodded. "A son. Irving. Lousy name, but it was the one uncle he had on her side who had money. Not that it got us or him anything. I love him, but I almost never see him."

"Because you're on the road?"

"Naw. You'd be surprised what you can work. I'm supposed to have visitation rights, but somehow he's always away when I come visiting. She don't want him to see me, get to know me instead of her current as his daddy. Uh-uh."

"Couldn't you go to court on that?"

He laughed. "Honey, them courts will slap me in jail so fast if I miss a payment to her it isn't funny—but tell *her* to live up to *her* end of the bargain? Yeah, they'll tell her, and that's that. Tell her and tell her and tell her. Until, one day, you realize that the old joke's true—she got the gold mine in the settlement and I got the shaft. Oh I suppose I could make an unholy mess trying to get custody, but I'd never win. I'd have to give up truckin', and truckin's all I know how to do. And I'd probably lose, anyway—nine out of ten men do. Even if I won—hell, it's been near five years." He sighed. "I guess at this stage he's better off. I hope so."

"I hope so, too," she responded, sounding genuinely touched, with the oddly pleasing guilt felt when, sunk deep in self-pity, you find a fellow sufferer.

They rode in near silence for the next few minutes, a silence broken only by the occasional crackle from the CB and a report of this or that or two jerks talking away at each other when they could just as easily have used a telephone and kept the world out.

Finally he said, "I guess from what you say that your marriage didn't work out either."

"Yeah, you could say that. He was an Air Force sergeant at Lackland. A drill instructor in basic. We met in a bar and got drunk on the town. He was older and a very lonely man, and, well, you know what I was going through. We just kinda fell into it. He was a pretty rough character, and after all the early fun had worn off and we'd settled down, he'd come home at night and take all his frustrations out on me. It really got to him, after a while, that I was smarter and better educated than he was. He had some inferiority complex. He was hell on his recruits, too—but they got away from him after eight weeks or so. I had him for years. After a while he got transferred up to Reese in Lubbock, but he hated that job and he hated the cold weather and the dust and wind, and that just made it all the worse. Me, I had it really bad there, too, since what few friends I had were all in San Antonio."

"I'd have taken a hike long before," he commented. "Divorce ain't all that bad. Ask my ex."

"Well, it's easy to see that—now. But I had some money for the first time, and a house, and a real sense of something permanent, even if it was lousy. I know it's kind of hard to understand—it's hard to explain. I guess you just had to be me. I figured maybe kids would mellow him out and give me a new direction—but after two miscarriages, the second one damn near killing me, the doctors told me I should never have kids. Probably couldn't but definitely shouldn't. That just made him meaner and sent me down the tubes. Booze, pot, pills—you name it, I swallowed it or smoked it or sniffed it. And one day—it was my thirtieth birthday—I looked at myself in the mirror, saw somebody a shot-to-hell forty-five looking back at me, picked up what I could use most and carry easy, cashed a check for half our joint account, and took a bus south to think things out. I've been walking ever since— and I still haven't been out of the goddamned state of Texas. I waited tables, swept floors, never stayed long in one spot. Hell, I've sold my body for a plate of eggs. Done everything possible to keep from thinking, looking ahead, worrying. I burned out. I've had it."

He thought about it for a moment, and then it came to him. "But you jumped out of that fella's car."

She nodded wearily. "Yeah, I did. I don't even know why, exactly. Or maybe, yes, I do, too. It was an all-of-a-sudden kind of thing, sort of like when I turned thirty and looked in the mirror. There wasn't any mirror, really, but back there in that car I still kind of looked at myself and was, well, scared, frightened, maybe even revolted at what I saw staring back. Something just sorta said to me, 'If this is the rest of your life, then why bother to be alive at all?'"

He thought, but could find little else to say right then. What *was* the right thing to say to somebody like this, anyway?

Flecks of rain struck his windshield, and he flipped on the wipers, the sound adding an eerie, hypnotic background to the sudden roar of a midsummer thunderstorm on a truck cab. Peering out, he thought for a moment he saw two Interstate 10 roadways—an impossible sort of fork he knew just couldn't be there. He kicked on the brights and the fog lights, and the image seemed to resolve itself a bit, the right-hand one looking more solid. He decided that keeping to the white stripe down the side of the road separating road and shoulder was the safest course.

At the illusory intersection, there seemed for a moment to be two trucks, one coming out of the other, going right, while the other, its ghostly twin, went left. The image of the second truck, apparently passing his and vanishing quickly in the distance to his left, startled him for a moment. He could have sworn there wasn't anything behind him for a couple of miles, and the CB was totally silent.

The rain stopped as suddenly as it had begun, and things took on a more normal appearance in minutes. He glanced over at the woman and saw that she was asleep—best thing for her, he decided. Ahead loomed a green exit sign, and, still a little unnerved, he badly wanted to get his bearings.

The sign said, "Ruddygore, 5 miles."

That didn't help him much. Ruddygore? Where in hell was that? The next exit should be Sheffield. A mile marker approached, and he decided to check things out.

The little green number said, "4."

He frowned again, beginning to become a little unglued. Four? That couldn't be right. Not if he was still on I-10. Uneasily, he began to think of that split back there. Maybe it *was* a split—that other truck had seemed to curve off to the left when he went right. If so, he was on some cockeyed interstate spur to God knew where.

God knew, indeed. As far as *he* knew or could remember, there were no exits, let alone splits, between Ozona and Sheffield.

He flicked on his interior light and looked down at his road atlas, held open by clips to the west Texas map. According to it, he was right—and no sign of any Ruddygore. He sighed and snapped off the light. Well, the thing was wrong in a hundred places, anyway. Luckily he was still ahead of schedule, so a five-mile detour shouldn't be much of a problem. He glanced over to his left again for no particular reason. Funny. The landscaping made it look as if there weren't any lane going back.

A small interstate highway marker, the usual red, white, and blue was between mile markers 3 and 2, but it told him nothing. It didn't even make sense. He was probably just a little crazy tonight, or his eyes were going, but it looked for all the world as if it said:

∞? What the hell was *that*? Somebody in the highway department must have goofed good there, stenciling an 8 on its side.

At the 2, another green sign announced Ruddygore, and there was also a brown sign, like the kind used for parks and monuments. It said, "Ferry—Turn Left at Stop Sign."

Now he knew he had gone suddenly mad. Not just that he knew that I-8 went from Tucson to San Diego and nowhere near Texas, but—a ferry? In the middle of the west Texas desert?

He backed down to slow—very slow—and turned to his passenger. "Hey, little lady. Wake up!"

She didn't stir, and finally he reached over and shook her, repeating his words.

She moved and squirmed and managed to open her eyes. "Um. Sorry. So *tired*...What's the matter? We in El Paso?"

He shook his head. "No. I think I've gone absolutely nuts. Somehow in the storm we took an exit that wasn't supposed to be there and we're headed for a town called Ruddygore. Ever heard of it?"

She shook her head sleepily from side to side. "Nope. But that doesn't mean anything. Why? We lost?"

"Lost ain't the word," he mumbled. "Look, I don't want to scare you or anything, but I think I'm going nuts. You ever hear of a ferryboat around here?"

She looked at him as if he had suddenly sprouted feathers. "A what? Over *what*?"

He nodded nervously and gestured toward the windshield. "Well, then, you read me that big sign."

She rubbed the sleep from her eyes and looked. "Ruddygore—exit one mile," she mumbled.

"And the little brown sign?"

"Ferry," she read, suddenly awake and looking very confused. "And an arrow." She turned and faced him. "How long was I asleep?"

"Five, maybe ten minutes," he answered truthfully. "You can see the rain on the windshield where the wipers don't reach."

She shook her head in wonder. "It must be across the Pecos. But the Pecos isn't much around here."

"Yeah," he replied and felt for his revolver.

The interstate road went right into the exit, allowing no choice. There was a slight downgrade to a standard stop sign and a set of small signs. To the left, they said, were Ruddygore and the impossible ferry. To the right was— Oblivion.

"I never heard of any town named Oblivion, either," he muttered, "but it sounds right for these parts. Still, all the signs said only Ruddygore, so that's got to be the bigger and closer place. Any place they build an interstate spur to at a few million bucks a mile *has* to have something open even at this time of night. Besides," he added, "I'm damned curious to see that ferry in the middle of the desert."

He put on his signals, then made the turn onto a modest two-lane road. He passed under the highway and noted glumly that there wasn't any apparent way of getting back on. Well, he told himself, he'd find it later.

Up ahead in the distance he saw, not the town lights he'd expected, but an odd, circular, lighted area. It was particularly unusual in that it looked something like the kind of throw a huge spotlight, pointed straight down, might give—but there were no signs of light anywhere. Fingering the pistol, he proceeded on, knowing that the road was leading him to that lighted area.

And it *was* bright when he reached it, although no source was apparent. The road, too, seemed to vanish into it, and the entire surface appeared as smooth as glass. Damnedest thing he'd ever seen, maybe a thousand yards across. He stopped at the edge of it, and both he and the woman strained to see where the light was coming from, but the sky remained black—blacker than usual, since the reflected glow blotted out all but the brightest stars.

"Now, what the hell...?" he mused aloud.

"Hey! Look! Up ahead there, almost in the middle. Isn't that a man?" She pointed through the windshield.

He squinted and nodded. "Yeah. Sure looks like somebody. I don't like this, though. Not at all. There's some very funny game being played here." Again he reached in and felt the comfort of the .38 in his pocket. He put the truck back in gear and moved slowly forward, one eye on the strange figure ahead and the other warily on the woman, whom he no longer trusted. It was a great sob story, but this craziness had started only after she came aboard.

He drove straight for the lone figure standing there in the center of the lighted area at about five miles per hour, applying the hissing air brakes when he was almost on top of the stranger and could see him clearly.

The woman gasped. "He looks like a vampire Santa Claus!"

Her nervous surprise seemed genuine. Certainly her description of the man who stood looking back at them fitted him perfectly. Very tall—six-five or better, he guessed—and very large. "Portly" would be too kind a word. The man had a reddish face, twinkling eyes with laugh lines etched around them, and a huge, full white beard—the very image of Santa Claus on all those Christmas cards. But he was not dressed in any furry red suit, but rather in formal wear—striped pants, morning coat, red velvet vest and cummerbund, even a top hat, and he was also wearing a red-velvet-lined opera cape.

The strange man made no gestures or moves, and finally the driver said, "Look, you wait in the truck. I'm going to find out what the hell this is about."

"I'm coming with you."

"*No!*" He hesitated a moment, then nervously cleared his throat. "Look, first of all, if there's any danger I don't want you between me and who I might have to shoot—understand? And second, forgive me, but I can't one hundred percent trust that you're not in on whatever this is."

That last seemed to shock her, but she nodded and sighed and said no more.

He opened the door, got down, and put one hand in his pocket, right on the trigger. Only then did he walk forward toward the odd figure who stood there, to stop a few feet from the man. The stranger said nothing, but the driver could feel those eyes following his every move and gesture.

"Good morning," he opened. What else was there to say to start things off?

The man in the top hat didn't reply immediately, but seemed to examine him from head to toe as an appraiser might look at a diamond ring. "Oh, yes, you'll do nicely, I think," he said in a pleasant, mellow voice with a hint of a British accent. He looked up at the woman, still in the cab, seemingly oblivious to the glare of the truck lights. "She, too, I suspect, although I really wasn't expecting her. A pleasant bonus."

"Hey, look, you!" the driver called angrily, losing patience. "What the hell *is* all this?"

"Oh, dear me, forgive my manners!" the stranger responded. "But, you see, *you* came *here*, I didn't come to you. Where do you *think* you are—and where do you want to be?"

Because the man was right, it put the driver on the defensive. "Uh, um, well, I seem to have taken a bum turn back on Interstate 10. I'm just trying to get back to it."

The big man smiled gently. "But you never *left* that road. You're still on it. You'll be on it for another nineteen minutes and eighteen seconds."

The driver just shook his head disgustedly. He must be as nutty as he looked, that was for sure. "Look, friend. I got stuck over here by accident in a thunderstorm and followed the road back there to—what was the town? Oh, yeah, Ruddygore. I figure I'll turn around there. Can you just tell me how far it is?"

"Oh, Ruddygore isn't an 'it,' sir," the strange man replied. "You see, *I'm* Ruddygore. Throckmorton P. Ruddygore, at your service." He doffed his top hat and made a small bow. "At least, that's who I am when I'm here."

The driver gave an exasperated sigh. "Okay, that's it. Forget it, buddy. I'll find my own way back."

"The way back is easy, Joe," Ruddygore said casually. "Just follow the road back. But you'll die, Joe—nineteen minutes eighteen seconds after you rejoin your highway. A second storm with hail and a small twister is up there, and it's going to cause you to skid, jackknife, then fall over into a gully. The overturning will break your neck."

He froze, an icy chill going through him. "How did you know my name was Joe?" His hand went back to the .38.

"Oh, it's my business to know these things," the strange man told him. "Recruiting is such a problem with many people, and I must be very limited and very selective for complicated reasons."

Suddenly all his mother's old legends about conjure men and the demons of death came back from his childhood, where they'd been buried for perhaps forty years—and the childhood fears that went with them returned as well, although he hated himself for it. "Just who—or what—*are* you?"

"Ruddygore. Or a thousand other names, none of which you'd recognize, Joe, I'm no superstition and I'm no angel of death, any more than that truck radio of yours is a human mouth. I'm not causing your death. It is preordained. It cannot be changed. I only know about it—found out about it, you might say—and am taking advantage of that knowledge. That's the hard part, Joe. Finding out. It costs me greatly every time I try and might just kill *me* someday. Compared with that, diverting you here to me was child's play." He looked up at the woman, who was still in the cab, straining to hear. "Shall we let the lady join us?"

"Even if I buy what you're saying—which I don't," Joe responded, "how does she fit in? Is she going to die, too?"

The big man shrugged. "I haven't the slightest idea. Certainly she'll be in the accident, unless you throw her out ahead of time. I expected you to be alone, frankly."

Joe pulled the pistol out and pointed it at Ruddygore. "All right. Enough of this. I think maybe you'll tell me what this all is, really, or I'll put a hole in you. You're pretty hard to miss, you know."

Ruddygore looked pained. "I'll thank you to keep my weight out of this. As for what's going on—I've just told you."

"You've told me nothing! Let's say what you say is for real, just for the sake of argument. You say I'm not dead yet, and you're no conjure spirit, so you pulled me off the main line of my death for something. What?"

"Oh, I didn't say I wasn't involved in magic. Sorcery, actually. That's what I do for a living. I'm a necromancer. A sorcerer." He shrugged. "It's a living—and it pays better than truck driving."

The pistol didn't waver. "All right. You say I'm gonna die in—I guess fifteen minutes or less now, huh?"

"No. Time has stopped for you. It did the moment you diverted to my road. It will not resume until you return to the Interstate, I think you called it."

"So we just stand here and I live forever, huh?"

"Oh, my, no! I have important things to do. I must be on the ferry when it comes. When I leave you'll be back on that road instantly, deciding you just had a nutty dream—for nineteen minutes eighteen seconds, that is."

Joe thought about it. "And suppose I do a flip, don't keep going west? Or suppose I exit at Fort Stockton? Or pull over the side for a half hour?"

Ruddygore shrugged. "What difference? You wouldn't know if that storm was going to hit you hard because you were sitting by the side of the road or because you turned back—you can never be sure. I am. You can't avoid it. Whatever you do will take you to your destiny."

Joe didn't like that. He also didn't like the fact that he was taking this all so seriously. It was just a funny man in a circle of—"Where does the light come from?"

"I create it. For stuff like this, I like to work in a spotlight. I'll turn it off if you like." He snapped his fingers, and suddenly the only lights were the truck headlights and running lights, which still illuminated Ruddygore pretty well.

Suddenly the vast sea of stars that was the west Texas sky on a clear night faded in, brilliant and impressive and, somehow, reassuring.

Joe heard the door open and close on the passenger side and knew that the woman was coming despite his cautions. He couldn't really blame her—hell, this was crazy.

"What's going on?" she wanted to know.

Ruddygore turned, bowed low, and said, "Madam, it is a pleasure to meet you, even if you are an unexpected complication. I am Throckmorton P. Ruddygore."

She stared at him, then over at Joe, half in shadow, and caught sight of the pistol in his hand. "Hey—what's this all about?" she called to him, disturbed.

"The man says I'm dead, honey," Joe told her. "He says I'm about to have a fatal accident. He says he's a conjure man. Other than that, he's said nothing at all."

Her mouth opened, then closed and she looked confusedly from one man to the other. She was not a small woman, but she felt dwarfed by the two giants. Finally she said to Ruddygore, "Is he right?"

Ruddygore nodded. "I'm afraid so. Unless, of course, he takes me up on my proposition."

"I figured we'd get to the point of all this sooner or later," Joe muttered.

"Exactly so," Ruddygore agreed. "I'm a recruiter, you see. I come from a place that's not all *that* unfamiliar to people of your world, but which is, in effect, a world of its own. It is a world of men—and others—both very much like and very different from what you know. It is a world both more peaceful and more violent than your Earth. That is, there are no guns, no nuclear missiles, no threats of world holocaust. The violence is more direct, more basic—say medieval. Right now that world is under attack and it needs help. After examining all the factors, I find that help from outside my world might—*might*—have a slight edge, for various reasons too long to go into here. And so I look for recruits, but not just *any* recruits. People with special qualities that will go well over there. People who fit special requirements to do the job. And, of course, people who are about to die and who meet those other requirements are the best recruits. You see?"

"Let me get this straight," the woman put in. "You're from another planet?" She looked up at the stars. "Out there? And you're whisking away people to help you fight a war? And we've got the chance to join up and go—or die?"

"That's about the size of it," Ruddygore admitted. "Although you are not quite right. First of all, I have no idea if *you* will die. I had no idea you would be in the truck. And, as an honorable man, I must admit that he might be able to save you if, after returning to the road, he lets you off. Might. He, however, *is* in the situation you describe. Secondly, I'm no little green man from Mars. The world I speak of is not up *there*, it's—well, somewhere else." He looked thoughtful for a moment.

"Think of it this way," he continued. "Think of opposites. Nature usually contains opposites. There is even, I hear, a different kind of matter, anti-matter, that's as real as we are yet works so opposite to us that, if it came into contact with us, it would cancel itself and us out. When the Earth was created, my world was also created—a by-product you might say, of the creation. It's very much like Earth, but it is in many ways an opposite. It runs by different rules. But it's as real a place as any you've been to, and, I think, a better, nicer place than Earth in a number of ways."

Far off in the distance there seemed to come a deep sound, like a boat's whistle, or a steam train blowing off. Ruddygore heard it and turned back to Joe.

"You have to decide soon, you know," he told the driver. "The ferry's coming in, and it won't wait long. Although few ride it, because only a few can find it or even know of it, it keeps a rigid schedule, for the path it travels is impossible unless you're greatly skilled *and* well timed. You can die and pass beyond my ken to the unknown beyond, or you can come with me. Face it, Joe. What have you got to lose? Even if you somehow could beat your destiny, you're only going through the motions, anyway. There's nothing for you in *this* world anymore. I offer a whole new life."

"And maybe just as short," the driver replied. "I did my bit of soldiering."

"Oh, it's not like that. We have many for armies. I need you for special tasks, not military ones. Adventure, Joe. A new life. A new world. I will make you young again. Better than you ever were."

Something snapped inside the driver. "No! You're Satan come to steal me at the last minute! I know you now!" And, with that, he fired three shots point-blank at Ruddygore.

The huge man didn't even flinch, but simply smiled, pursed his lips, and spat out the three spent bullets. "Lousy aim," he commented. "I really didn't catch any of them. I had to use magic." He sighed sadly. The whistle sounded again, closer now. "But I'm not the devil, Joe. I'm flesh and blood and I live. I am not a man, but I was once a man, and still am more than not. There are far worse things than your silly, primitive devil, Joe—that's part of what I'm fighting. Come with me—now. Down to the dock.

Joe looked disgusted, both with Ruddygore and with the pistol. "All right, Ruddygore, or whoever or whatever you are. It don't make any difference, anyway. I can't go. Not if I can save her. You understand the duty."

Ruddygore nodded sadly. "I feared as much when I saw her in the cab. And for such a motive I can't stop you or blame you. Damn! You wouldn't believe how much trouble all this was, too. What a waste."

"Hey! Wait a minute!" the woman put in. "Don't *I* get to say anything about this?"

They both looked at her expectantly.

"Look, if I had a million bucks, I'd bet that I'm still sound asleep in that truck up there, speeding down a highway toward El Paso, and that this is all a crazy dream. But it's a great dream. The best I ever had. I'm on my way to kill myself. I've had it—up to here. I gave up on this stupid, crazy world. So I'm dreaming—or I'm psycho, in some funny world of my own. Okay. I'll take it. It's better than real life. There's no way I'm going back to that lie. No way I'm getting back in that truck, period. I've finally done it! Gone completely off my rocker into a fantasy world that sounds pretty good to me."

Ruddygore's face broke into a broad, beaming smile. He looked over at the driver. "Joe? What do you say now?"

"Well, I heard her story and I can't say I blame her. But I'm the one who's gone bananas, not her."

"Dreams," Ruddygore mused. "No, this is no dream, but think of it that way if you like. For, in a sense, we're all just dreams. The Creator's dreams. And where we travel to is out there." He gestured with a cane, gold-tipped and with a dragon's head for a handle. "Out across the Sea of Dreams and beyond to the far shore. So take it as a dream, the both of you, if you wish. As a dream, you have even less to lose."

The pistol finally went down and was replaced in Joe's pocket. He looked back at the truck. "Maybe we should get our things."

"You won't need them," Ruddygore told him. "All will be provided to you as you need it. That's part of the bargain." The whistle sounded a third time, very close now, and Ruddygore turned to face the dark direction of its cry. "Come. Just follow me."

Joe looked back at his truck again. "I should at least kill the motor and the lights," he said wistfully. "That truck's the only thing I got, the only thing I ever had in my whole life that was real. This ferry—I don't suppose...?"

Ruddygore shook his head sadly. "No, I'm afraid not. Your truck wouldn't work over there. The captain would never allow it, anyway, because we couldn't get it off the boat and it would take up too much room. But don't worry about it, Joe. It's not really here, you see. It's somewhere back there, on your Interstate 10."

With that the truck faded and was gone, lights, engine, noise, and all, and they were in total darkness.

The whistle sounded once more, and it seemed almost on top of them.

MY LIFE AS A MERMAID

Jen Grow was an undergraduate at Towson University when her creative writing teacher, George Friedman, brought Anne Tyler to class to read and answer questions. Jen recalls that time with Anne Tyler as a defining moment for a young student writer who hoped someday to publish her own work—and publish she did. Jen's story collection, My Life as a Mermaid, *was winner of the 2012 Dzanc Books Short Story Collection Competition. She is the Fiction Editor of* Little Patuxent Review. *Her short fiction and nonfiction have appeared in* The Writer's Chronicle, Other Voices, The Sun, *the* GSU Review, Hunger Mountain, Indiana Review *and many others. She co-authored the book* Seeking the Spirit *(Morehouse Publishing, 2006) with Harry Brunett. She received two Individual Artist Awards from the Maryland State Arts Council and her stories have earned nominations for Best New American Voices and a Pushcart Prize.*

———————

I get another letter from my sister who is in Honduras riding mules and skidding around the muddy mountain roads in a pickup truck. The roads have curves sharp enough to invite death, sharp enough to see yourself leaving. When the priest drives, she writes, he is the real danger, his faith too strong to be cautious. My sister, Kay, has learned to hope for days when the truck breaks down. Otherwise, she and the other relief workers cower in the open bed as the priest speeds through the countryside; they lean all their weight toward the mountain to keep the truck from sliding off the washed-out roads. Some days they leave their base camp and carry their supplies up the mountains by foot. They pack Tylenol, Imodium, vitamins. And antibiotics: Keflex, Pen-VK, Erythromycin, Lorabid, Roxar, tubes of anti-fungal cream, and everything for parasites.

Me, I stock up on Band-Aids and Flintstones chewables as I wheel my cart down the pharmacy aisle. Suntan lotion, cotton balls, hairspray, toothpaste. I gather toilet paper and paper towels—the jumbo pack—for all the spills I wipe. Would a sponge work better, save some trees? my sister might ask. But I am one to leave the sponge in the sink, smelly and sour, until the odor clings to my hands and infects everything I try to clean. "That wouldn't happen if you squeezed it out every time," my husband instructs all of us, the kids included. He demonstrates his method over the sink, a surplus of gray water drizzling from the sponge, an army of germs exterminated. "Squeeze out all the extra," he says. I nod. The kids have lost interest. Still, I prefer paper towels. They absorb everything. Plus, there's the satisfaction of throwing them out—the illusion of messes going away.

***

In her letter, Kay says there's no indoor plumbing. No showers, no tubs. Toilets that do not flush "as you know it," she says, to emphasize the differences between us. On the other hand, she says, there is plenty of water. It rains daily for an hour or more. She washes in a pan of rainwater, one leg at a time, and keeps her bar of soap, gray and shrinking, in a

Ziploc baggie. The Ziploc has become valuable, irreplaceable, and she folds it neatly to preserve it.

When her team of eight (the priest, a couple of saints, a paramedic, a skittish med student, and a teenage interpreter, plus bodyguards strapped in bullets) hikes back, exhausted from a day in the mountains, a day of shouting "Atención! Atención!" through a bullhorn to the trees, announcing the arrival of "medico" to treat infected hands and swollen limbs that should be amputated, diarrhea of all types, pneumonia, chicken pox, dengue, skin fungus, worms, and clogged ears—when she's finished distributing whatever antibiotics are left to treat the sexual diseases and parasites buried deep within the bodies of these people, my sister carries her bucket of rainwater to her stucco cell, where she soaps herself a leg at a time, an arm, a shoulder, trying to remove the day's dust and sorrow. The stench of sulfur water is not much better than the decay she's wiping clean.

Afterward, she gathers her clothes and scrubs and wrings them in her bathwater and hangs them to dry. Then she uses the twice-dirty water to flush her toilet in the corner of her cell. She says she has not yet gotten used to the sourness that consumes her hair and skin and clothes. "How does a thing become so soiled? So black and unwanting of touch?" she asked in her letter. I don't know if she is referring to her cell or toilet or the countryside in general. I cannot answer, having never witnessed a thing so dirty as to be mourned.

***

Many years ago, we were two girls swimming in the ocean every summer. Family vacations, sand and sunburn, salty waves. If not the ocean, we swam in the pool until our lips turned blue. We knew how to make our bodies float or sink, how to dive away from our mother's voice when she pleaded with us to get out. "Girls!" she'd yell. "Girls, I'm warning you, if I have to pull you out myself!" Kay and I would plunge even deeper and isolate ourselves in the silence of the water. We taught ourselves to jump waves, to dive, to hold tea parties underwater until our bodies floated upward and our lungs ran out of air.

I have tried to teach this trick to my own children along with underwater handstands and somersaults, but my children do not swim like me. They have inherited their father's fear. They keep to the shallow end and drift to the sides. My youngest child is afraid to get his face wet, a screamer if he is splashed, hyperventilating until his face is red and purple. When this happens, I hold him close to my chest and gently glide back and forth in the water. But this has never soothed him as it does me. He is most happy playing on the grass, where his feet feel sure of the world beneath him.

There are other children at the community pool who dive deep and search the bottom. Their parents call them fish or mermaids. Lovely swimmers. But they do not belong to me.

***

On sunny afternoons in my suburban home I worry about my kids, my sister, the world. I fear catastrophe. I'd like to write Kay and ask her how she escaped these worries, but instead I write short letters begging her to be careful. Then I forget to mail them and use the envelopes as a place to jot down my list of things to do:

go to post office/ bank
laundry
call therapist

get aspirin, ice cream, Diet Coke

nap

I fuss over my children in the same distracted, heartsick way while I count the tiny pairs of socks that come out of the dryer. I fold their miniature clothes into piles. Some days I feel like Gulliver, every part of me tied down by Lilliputians, as if, somehow, it is me and not my sister who has wandered into a strange land. The land of marriage, motherhood, matching socks. It's not what I expected. How did I choose this, wandering the grocery store with my squeaky cart? Nor is it clear how my sister escaped to Honduras. It seems impossible that all these worlds are connected, the past with the present, Honduras with here. Though in some ways, it could be as simple as purchasing an airline ticket and trusting the winds of God—the whims of God—to land in a small pocket between the slopes of two mountains, like finding shelter between the breasts of a giant mother.

Kay flew to Honduras after a devastating hurricane ripped through the country. The hospital in Tegucigalpa was flooded four stories high. Rushing water sucked bodies away from the villages, depositing death everywhere like sediment. I know this not from the news, which focused on wealthier parts of the world, but from my sister and her small band of relief workers. They flew into a smelly tropical world for various reasons, among them compassion and the longing for a place to hide.

Kay writes, "I took a rare dip in one of the rivers today, surrounded by mangrove trees. I floated in smooth brown water where I wanted to live forever as a fish." I'm envious. I would run away; I would like to be the kind of person who could run away.

***

Some days I feel like I am at the bottom of an empty aquarium watching the world through a glass wall. The floor of my aquarium is covered with toys that have fallen apart or have missing pieces. "Somebody has to clean this up!" I yell to my children, who are upstairs in their rooms hiding from my voice. When no one comes, I bend down and straighten the mess myself. Pick up the pieces and put them in a pile.

I ask, How on earth can I, from here, straighten up the world? Absorb all the spills? Know in some concrete way how wasteful my wanting is? Every few weeks, I write out another twenty-dollar check to Unicef or the Fireman's Fund, the Police Youth camp, the world food bank. I stuff my checks into their pre-addressed envelopes and then I forget to mail them.

"Don't you think we could do something?" I say to my husband at night in bed. I sound like one of the children pleading to keep a stray kitten.

"You're suffering from guilt," my husband tells me. "Did you call your therapist?"

It's not guilt, I want to explain. It's something else. But my husband is a giant wall of a man whose back is turned to me. I draw invisible circles on his skin.

"Go ahead and deny yourself," he says. "But not the rest of us." He's fed up with the diet of rice and onions I've been serving for dinner lately.

"This is what your Aunt Kay is eating tonight, so lick your bowls!" I tell the kids. They love the idea of eating with their fingers. "In other parts of the world people are starving," I remind them when they spit out the onions.

"We are civilized in this household. We will use forks," my husband says, too late to stop the chaos at the dinner table.

"What about pizza, Daddy?" one of the kids asks. "We eat that with our hands."

All of us except my husband scoop rice with our fingers, we lick and gobble like the dogs we are. This is play for the children, not a state of being. I cannot replicate the poverty of the world so anyone will believe me, fold hunger back on itself. I cannot pretend I am anywhere but here. We eat mangoes and bananas for dessert. Ice cream. The kids think life's a picnic because we've been eating off paper plates. Since the drought this summer and the state's call to conserve, I've stopped doing dishes. We haven't hooked the hose to the lawn sprinkler, washed the cars, or turned on the birdbath fountain for weeks. My husband thinks this is enough sacrifice. Every evening, he studies the landscaping, which cost a fortune, and the browning lawn. Then he looks at the sky, waiting. I've been making the children bathe at the same time. Three at once is harder to handle, all the splashing and name-calling, the middle child squished in between. After their baths, we scoop the tub water into pots and carry the containers downstairs to soak the houseplants. We drip all the way to the herb garden out back and make circles of mud around the wildflowers and tomato plants. My clean-scrubbed kids parade in their pajamas; gray water the color of old soap dripping down their arms. Really, there is more dirty water than I know what to do with.

***

I tell them I'm going to the store to buy jugs of water, that I will be back soon. I buy ice cream instead. I buy ice cream regularly these last few months, and each time I drive a little bit farther, looking for a different store, another flavor. We've hoarded several cartons of ice cream at home, gallons of water, so it isn't a need I'm chasing. Water is just my flimsy excuse to get away.

Lately, I've been taking refuge in the grocery store. I wheel up and down the aisles, amazed by the abundance. I study the shelves of canned vegetables, rows of soup. "Excuse me," I hear a woman ask the clerk. "Can you tell me where to find artichokes?"

She pronounces it "heart-a-choke," and I think, "They're everywhere. Poor choking hearts." For instance, this one: Kay wrote me about a woman with mastitis. The woman had a giant sloughing pit of a breast, a hollow where her body used to be. The worst case Kay's ever seen. I cannot picture it, except as black ash. A side of a woman ready to blow away.

Tonight, I finger the fresh produce. I stop my cart next to a bin of corn on the cob and pick out an ear. I pull back the husk and part the silk—the kids call it Barbie hair. They love to play with corn silk Barbie. Beautiful Barbie. Except squirming underneath the Barbie hair is a fat worm tunneling its way through the ear of corn. Even the worms of this country eat well. I think of the Honduran children Kay wrote about, some of whom had worms sprouting from their foreheads. The torsala flies that are everywhere in Honduras circle the children's heads like black halos. When the children are napping, the flies bite their foreheads and lay eggs. The larvae hatch from swollen pouches. Kay says it's a horrific sight, but not life-threatening, easy enough to treat with antibiotics and creams. How can worms bursting from a child's forehead not be threatening to life? To my life? I am haunted by these images when I bathe my children at night, their skin glowing gorgeous, as smooth as perfect fresh peaches, which, I notice, are on sale. I pick out a half-dozen flawless fruits and admire the beauty of things grown without deformities.

At night, when I count my children and make sure all are safe and sleeping, when I lie in bed with my husband and stare at his back, I think of letters I'll write my sister. "When you are taking care of other people's children," I'll ask her, "who do you count as belonging to you?"

I leave the grocery store with a gallon of water, a carton of ice cream, the peaches, and a bundle of paper towels. Weaving through the parking lot, I see myself in someone's side-view mirror, my hair in my eyes, my French twist loose and lopsided, my arm stretched around the jumbo paper towels. I balance them on my hip as if I am carrying one more child, the child who will clean up the world, wipe up the spills, absorb it all.

I carry my groceries through the parking lot, and then, before I move in time, an old woman backs her car into my hip. "Hey!" I yell. I pound my fist on her trunk and drop my bags. She's wearing a feathered hat and cannot fully turn her neck to see me. "Is that a condition of old age or of life—the not turning to see?" I want to ask. But the peaches are rolling across the asphalt, and the plastic jug has split. Clean, clear water seeps from the burst seam, forming small puddles and soaking the pavement like a stain. I can see the old woman's hands tremble on the steering wheel. She must be somebody's mother. I can tell she would like to help me pick up my groceries but doesn't know how. She cannot move from inside the safe bubble of her car except to wave and say she's sorry.

STATE FARM

Dave Housley's third collection of short fiction, If I Knew the Way, I Would Take You Home, *was published in 2015 by Dzanc Books. He is the author of* Commercial Fiction *(Outpost 19 Books), a book in which he wrote short stories based on television commercials ("State Farm" is a part of this ongoing project) and* Ryan Seacrest is Famous *(Impetus Press, Dzanc Books eBook Reprint). He is one of the founding editors of Barrelhouse magazine, and a co-founder of the Conversations and Connections writer's conference. Sometimes he drinks boxed wine and tweets about the things on his television at @housleydave.*

Jake from State Farm hangs up the phone and hustles to the bathroom. He relieves his bladder, leans his head against the cool tile, and breathes a sigh of relief. The last client just kept on talking. Jake isn't even sure how they got started on boats, water skiing, and then some place called Lake Chautauqua, which he pictures as a combination of the lake in *On Golden Pond* and the television commercial where the girls in bikinis are water skiing. He is not sure what that commercial is for—raisins, maybe?—but the brunette looks like Cindy at twenty-two and he has a recording of an episode of *Bones* that he'll never erase so he can see that smile, that hair waving, any time he pleases.

They were going to go to the Dominican Republic for the honeymoon and he wonders if they would have had water skiing there. The serenity to accept the things I can't change, he thinks.

He finishes at the urinal and then moves into the stall, pulls down his pants, and sits on the toilet. It is the only place he can decompress, just be alone for a few minutes. No phone, no computer, no Mr. Hernandez spouting motivational phrases, no lonely man halfway across the country asking leading questions about boat insurance they both know he'll never need.

He wonders if he is going to the bathroom too much, what the right amount is, if his urine is too yellow or not yellow enough. He wonders about the cramps in his stomach, the little twitch that has started up in his left eye. Ever since the night shift, he feels a little sick all the time. He should cut down on coffee, eat better. He should do a lot of things but right now is about triage, taking care of himself and working through the steps. Meetings every afternoon. Work every night.

The last call took forty-five minutes. Jake has been doing this for only four months but he can tell the lonely people when he hears them: The whispers, the light jokes, and half-convincing attempts to seem interested in insurance. He is comfortable with his side of these conversations, safe in the confines of his script: "Yeah…wow…okay…really?...huh… interesting…okay, so your current plan…"

He checks Cindy's Facebook. She is trying some new food service and has been posting pictures of her meals. "Tilapia

Meunière with Moroccan-Spiced Lentils and Rainbow Chard" was tonight's dinner. He scrolls down. No check-ins or mentions of dates or other men. Nothing but images of chicken, fish, or beef atop a bed of vegetables or lentils or other things he can't quite name. He wonders if he could name them if he was drinking. He wonders if he would care more, or less.

Night shift has thrown the timing of his meals off. He's not sure whether he should have a sandwich before he starts or take a break in the middle of the shift, if he should have breakfast at breakfast or find a place where they'll give him a burger. But that might also be a place where they would give him a beer and that would be no good right now. Not just right now, he reminds himself. That would be no good.

He needs to get back to his desk before Mr. Hernandez notices he has been gone longer than five minutes. Mr. Hernandez is twenty-four and has visions of corner offices and corporate retreats. Mr. Hernandez just may realize these things and more, and Jake is not sure if he should be sad or angry or feel sorry for the young man, with his short sleeve shirts and Wal-Mart ties, the keys that jingle on his belt as he stalks the cubicle aisle. Jake regards his own Dockers and red State Farm shirt. He lifts the shirt and smells.

He has been talking to Cindy's mother, Ruth, who answers the phone even though her daughter would be furious. Jake has been making amends and so far it has been kind of bullshit—sorry I was hungover, sorry I wasn't there for you, sorry sorry sorry. He has been selling Ruth on the twelve-step business, though, working it like some of the older people at the meetings, the ones who have turned being an alcoholic into being a semi-professional public speaker. He is better at this than he is with the insurance. He is invested. He improvises, cries, prays, laughs, shares.

Making amends with Cindy may be the last time he ever sees her, or it might be the beginning of the part that will make all of it–the DUI and the meetings and parking his car in an emptying lot in a strip mall a half hour outside of Hartford, trudging in to work while the rest of the world is trudging out, talking to lonely strangers about insurance in the middle of night–somehow make sense.

The last caller's wife actually got on the phone and yelled at him. The first time that had ever happened. "She sounds hideous!" the wife said. She hung up the phone and Jake could feel the tenuous strand between them, two men play-acting a conversation about boat insurance in the middle of the night, peeling back toward him like a bungee cord suddenly released.

He googles Chautauqua. There is a lake there and it does look lovely, but nothing like Golden Pond. It is a big lake, built up, with smiling women drinking white wine, places where good looking people sit on decks in the sun and drink cocktails and laugh. There is an institution there. He briefly wonders what that means and then puts it out of his mind. He is sitting on a toilet in the middle of the night in a rented shirt and tomorrow afternoon he will drink tepid coffee at a meeting and whatever the Chautauqua Institution is, it is not a thing for him.

The bathroom door opens and he hears the rattle of Mr. Hernandez's keys, the water running, and then the hand dryer's roar. "Okay in there, buddy?" Mr. Hernandez says.

"Yep. Okay. Just..." Jake says. The bathroom door shuts and the keys jingle back toward the row of cubicles. It is 4:15

a.m. Soon the first inklings of sun will smudge the windows along the empty row of cubicles on the back wall, the day shift cubicles, and he will count down the hours and then the minutes until 6:00 a.m. He will go to Denny's and eat a Meat Lover's Omelette while he reads the sports page. He will watch the old men in their groups, carefully avoiding eye contact while he listens in to their light grousing about the Patriots or Medicare or their adult children. He will wipe his plate with his wheat toast, tip 5 percent and nod at the waitress, then go home and watch whatever *CSI* is on until he gets tired, and it will be fine. It will all be fine.

Jake from State Farm pulls up his pants and cinches his belt. He exits the stall. He goes back to work.

THE HOUSEWARMING

Ronald Malfi *is an award-winning author of thirteen novels, several novellas, and short stories in the horror, mystery, and thriller genres. His suspense novel* Little Girls *was released from Kensington Books in summer 2015.*

In 2009, his crime drama, Shamrock Alley, *won a Silver IPPY Award. In 2011, his ghost story/mystery novel,* Floating Staircase, *was a finalist for the Horror Writers Association Bram Stoker Award for best novel, received a Gold IPPY Award for best horror novel, and the Vincent Preis International Horror Award for the German translation. His novel* Cradle Lake *garnered him the Benjamin Franklin Independent Book Award (silver) in 2014, while* December Park, *his epic coming-of-age thriller, won the Beverly Hills International Book Award for suspense in 2015.*

Most recognized for his haunting, literary style and memorable characters, Malfi's dark fiction has gained acceptance among readers of all genres.

He was born in Brooklyn, New York in 1977, and eventually relocated to the Chesapeake Bay area, where he currently resides with his wife Debra (another Towson alum) and their two daughters, Madison and Hayden. He graduated from Towson University with a B.S. in English in 1999.

Mark and Lisa Schoenfield spent the afternoon preparing for the party.

They scurried about their spacious new home, making sure the floors were spotless and the large bay windows were free from smudges. Lisa prepared guacamole, miniature tacos (chicken, beef, and vegetarian), cocktail wieners wrapped in flaky croissants, fruit salad, a Caesar salad, and a variety of cookies fanned out like playing cards on a gorgeous Wedgwood serving tray. Mark made the liquor store run, and returned with a carton of assorted bottles and several cases of low-calorie beer. They squabbled playfully over what playlist to select on their shared iPod, with Lisa preferring classical selections to Mark's more modern pop sensibilities. In the end, they settled on a rotation of up-tempo jazz numbers, and finished preparing for the event amidst the brassy intonations of Coltrane and Davis.

Mark was forty-two years old, in good shape, and had all his hair and teeth. He was a musician by trade, having once toured the East Coast with a group who played original Americana in the styles of Springsteen, Mellencamp, and Seger, though for the past decade or so he had found a comfortable little niche composing and recording the scores for independent studio films. This afforded him the luxury of working from home, which made the soundproofed basement the biggest selling point of the new house, at least as far as he was concerned.

Lisa was thirty-eight and was in equally good shape as her husband. She maintained her figure with a steadfast regimen of aerobic exercises, proper dieting, and an overall positive outlook. She was an attorney who specialized in contract law, and she had recently taken a position with a downtown firm who lured her away from her previous employers with promises of partnership in the not-too-distant future. The new job was the reason for the relocation, and for the new house.

And the house itself? It was a neoclassical Victorian with great flow and four bedrooms at the end of a quaint suburban cul-de-sac. The lawns were blindingly green, the driveway like a black satin ribbon winding in serpentine fashion up the gradual incline of the property toward the two-car garage with the carriage-house lights. At the topmost roof, a weathervane fashioned in the shape of an archer's arrow spiraled lazily in the cool summer breeze. It was the first house the Schoenfields visited, and they had made their offer—quite a generous offer—the very next day.

Now, two weeks after they had moved in, the place had begun taking on some semblance of home. In tandem, Mark and Lisa had spent much of the previous week visiting their nearest neighbors, introducing themselves in their cheerful and overzealous way. The neighbors all seemed friendly enough, and pleased to have a seemingly normal-looking couple move into the neighborhood.

"We're having a housewarming party this weekend," Mark and Lisa would take turns saying, "and we'd love it if you'd come by."

Nearly everyone on the block agreed, and seemed enchanted by the prospect.

The first guests arrived that night at precisely eight o'clock. They were a young couple named Baum, the man in spectacles and the woman in a swoopy floral sundress.

"Hey," Mark said, fervently shaking the man's hand while grinning to beat the band. "Great! You guys are the first to arrive. Can I get you a drink?"

Mark fixed a vodka tonic for Mr. Baum and a glass of merlot for Mrs. Baum, which he handed off to the respective guests with his smile still firmly in place. In the parlor, Lisa raised the volume of the iPod in an effort to make the atmosphere livelier.

Soon after, more guests arrived. Mark immediately made no promises to himself that he would remember all the names of his visitors, though he did intend to conclude the evening having memorized the names of at least three of the couples. The Tohts, the Nancers, the O'Learys, the Smiths, the Barrows—they were all young and handsome and well-groomed and cheerful. Each time the doorbell went off—a plangent *cling-clong!* that sounded to the Schoenfields like a church bell—a new wave of bright faces filed into the foyer. Lisa was pleased to see that many of the women brought food. Mark was pleased to find that a number of the men brought liquor.

As is the custom at such events, the men eventually gravitated toward one end of the house and remained huddled in a tight little group away from the women. They clutched cans of beer or rocks glasses and spoke of the neighborhood's comings and goings with a sense of pride and stewardship Mark Schoenfield admired. They were straight enough to be proper but loose enough to laugh at the occasional crass joke, which endeared them all the more to Mark. When one of the wives swooped by, the respective husband would slip an arm around her waist and plant a quick little peck on her check.

Lisa led an expedition of inquisitive women through the house—up and down the stairs, in and out of all the rooms. Closet doors were opened and bathroom shower stalls were subjected to intrusive scrutiny. One woman even possessed the audacity to peer under the bed in the master bedroom. A few women marveled over what the Schoenfields had managed to do with the place in such a short amount of time.

"We've hardly begun," informed Lisa.

"Nonsense!" said a woman named Tracy Birch. "The place is lovely!"

"Hadn't any of you been in the house before, when the previous owners had lived here?" Lisa asked the gaggle of women.

"Of course, dear," said Sandy O'Leary, "but they had gotten so *old,* and their tastes were so *old.* It's good to have fresh young blood back on the street."

Downstairs, the men had become garrulous in the absence of women. Mark was pleased to fetch them drinks and returned to the parlor at one point balancing a bowl of guacamole in one hand, drinks in the other, and a bag of Tostitos wedged under one arm. The men applauded his foresight then tore into the bag of chips like a pride of lions descending on a carcass.

"Do you play golf?" asked Bob O'Leary.

"On occasion," Mark said.

Bob O'Leary beamed and clapped him on the forearm. "Brilliant! There's an exceptional course less that fifteen miles from here. It's right on the bay. Gorgeous!"

"Gorgeous," echoed Milton Underland, who stood close by, his mouth full of guacamole. He held a beer in each hand.

The doorbell stopped ringing, yet the guests continued to arrive. The Nevins, the Copelands, the Wintermeyers, the Joneses, the de Filippos. Mark took snapshot photos of each of their faces by blinking his eyes. *Gotcha.* Heavily perfumed women kissed him wetly on the cheek, their scents floral and fecund and delightful. Each man shook his hand while gripping his upper arm in a familiar but not unwelcomed embrace. Mark realized that it had been a long time—since college, maybe—that he'd had a group of male friends with which he could so casually bond.

At one point during the evening, Mark and Lisa bumped into each other in the hallway. The rooms were choked with people and there were more walking up the flagstone path, but they didn't care: they kissed, and it wasn't a brief and perfunctory act. It was meaningful. The stress of the move sloughed from Mark's flesh; the anxiety of switching jobs seemed to burn off Lisa's shoulders like steam off hot blacktop.

The Quindlands, the Hamms, the Dovers, the MacDonalds, the Kellers, a second pair of Smiths—they kept coming. In the kitchen, fresh plates of food replaced old ones. Beer coolers were replenished with new cans and bottles then covered in a shower of ice cubes.

"What is it that you do?" Ted Hamm asked him.

"I'm a musician," Mark explained. "I compose and record the soundtracks for indie films."

"Fantastic! Any films I would know?"

"The most recent was called *Oglethorpe and Company*," Mark said, though he confessed that it had had only minimal distribution. "The most popular is probably the *Sledge* series of films."

"You mean those over-the-top horror movies where all those nubile young waifs get clobbered by the masked maniac wielding a sledgehammer?" Ted Hamm's eyes blazed with what Mark interpreted as pure enchantment.

"Yes," Mark said. "Those films."

"I *love* them! I go hog-wild for those movies! They're so ridiculously bloody; I don't know whether to laugh or scream in terror."

"Thank you," Mark said, unsure if such a comment should be taken as a compliment or not, "but I didn't make the movies. Just the soundtracks."

Another man—someone Mark hadn't yet met—appeared beside Ted Hamm and began humming the discordant title theme from the *Sledge* series of films. Ted grinned, nodding like an imbecile at the man, then turned his blank and grinning face back to Mark.

"Yeah," Mark said. "That's it, all right."

One of the wives also appeared before him. She was a slim brunette in a stunning red dress. She addressed the small upright piano toward the rear of the parlor with beautifully manicured fingernails. "You must play it," she told him. "Oh, please?"

"Yes!" boomed Ted Hamm. "You must!"

It seemed that he was carried toward the piano on a wave of arms. Before being deposited onto the piano bench, some invisible pair of fingers administered a sharp pinch to his midsection. The keyboard cover was thrust open, revealing a mouthful of grinning alabaster teeth. Temporarily disoriented, Mark did not begin to play until some of the guests began humming the theme song. He came in midway through the second bar, his fingers first fumbling over the keys before finding their rhythm.

"There it is!" one of the men shouted. "You've got it now!"

Mark laughed and continued to play. It was all minor chord progressions and jangly high keys—a simple but recognizable melody that had helped secure the *Sledge* franchise some status among horror movie aficionados.

When he finished, the room applauded. Yet when he tried to get up, hands appeared on his back and shoulders, forcing him back down onto the piano bench.

"Please," a woman's voice pleaded. "Once more around the mulberry bush, Mark."

So he cracked his knuckles and played the piece again.

Meanwhile, in the kitchen, Lisa found herself listening to the neighborhood gossip with mild voyeuristic pleasure. Which husband was sleeping with which wife; whose children were just *awful brutes;* what local restaurants were known swingers' joints.

"Is it something you've ever done?" one of the women asked Lisa.

"You mean Mark and me?" Lisa said, hearing Mark at the piano in the next room the instant she spoke his name. "Have we ever…?"

"Not even once?" another woman asked. She was meatier than the others, with great silver streaks in her otherwise raven-colored hair.

"No," Lisa confessed. "Not even once."

"This is so distasteful," said a third woman. Lisa thought her name was Betsy. "Such talk. Who are we, anyway? This isn't *Desperate Housewives*, you know."

A few of the women chided Betsy, though good-naturedly.

Lisa heard the piano stop again…then start up a third time. The same tune. She recognized it as the theme from those horror movies Mark had composed.

The patio door off the kitchen slid open and two good-looking couples came in. They ignored Lisa, and went to embrace some of the other women gathered around the kitchen. All of a sudden, Lisa felt like a stranger in her own house, and in her own life.

"The house is beautiful!" said one of the new women. "We love what you've done with the place. Show us around?"

"Yes," said the other woman. "We'd love the grand tour."

Again, Lisa took the women in and out of rooms, down hallways, opened closet doors. One of the women seemed to take exceptional interest in the cleanliness of the toilets, stopping to peer down at her reflection simmering on the surface of the water in each bowl.

After a while, Lisa packed away the food, leaving only the desserts on the counter. She brewed some Sumatran coffee and decided to forgo her good china cups in favor of the Styrofoam ones Mark had picked up yesterday at the grocery store. There were too many people and she didn't have enough china to go around. As she handed out coffee to extended hands, her guests smiled warmly at her.

"We love what you and Mark have done with the house," Sheila Duggan said.

"Your taste is exquisite," Sallyanne Monroe said.

"Oh," Lisa said, "we've hardly had a chance to do a thing."

The Bostons, the Daleys, the Fritzes, the Loans filed into the house, cheery-faced and smelling of colognes, perfumes, deodorants.

In the parlor, Mark struggled up off the piano bench. More hands gripped him and tried to force him back onto the bench, but he slid sideways and marshalled decisively through the crowd. Several of the guests issued boos at his departure until someone else claimed the piano bench and began playing a fairly commendable rendition of Joplin's "Maple Leaf Rag."

Mark found Lisa in the doorway between the parlor and the kitchen, her back toward him. He sighed into her hair and muttered, "My fingers are burning."

Lisa turned...and it wasn't Lisa at all. Another woman in the same dress, her hair done up in a similar fashion. The strangeness of her appearance caused Mark to utter a small cry.

"Hello," she said, smiling prettily at him.

"I'm sorry. I thought you were my wife."

"She's delightful," said the woman. "You both are. Was that you on the piano just a moment ago?"

"It was."

"You play so well. You are a professional?"

"Yes, I am."

"So wonderful to have such a talented new couple join the community."

In the kitchen, Lisa waved to him over a sea of bobbing heads and grinning faces. Mark excused himself and navigated through the crowd until he reached his wife. She looked tired.

"Coffee?" she asked him.

"I'm too tired for coffee," he said, "if that makes any sense."

"They keep coming," she said.

"They love us," he responded, though without the satisfaction expected with such a sentiment.

In the parlor, "Maple Leaf Rag" segued into "The Entertainer." Voices boomed in pleasure. A few of the women in the kitchen began dancing with each other, their coffee cups held up above their heads while they twirled each other around with their free hands.

A perky redhead approached the Schoenfields dragging behind her a man in a pressed oxford shirt and pleated khakis. "My husband Michael and I missed the tour of the house," she said in a nasally, almost pleading voice. "Is it too late for us? We'd love to see all the work you've been doing."

"We really would," Michael added.

"We haven't done any work," Mark advised the couple.

"Everyone is bragging about the upstairs," said the woman, as if she hadn't heard him.

"It's nothing," Lisa cut in.

The redheaded woman cheered with glee, clasping her hands together. "I bet it's outstanding!"

Mark and Lisa exchanged a look. "I'll take them," he offered, then led the couple up the stairs. The three of them wandered around the hallway, dipping in and out of unfinished bedrooms, bathrooms, closets. The redhead paused before one bathroom mirror to examine her reflection, then— astoundingly—she readjusted her cleavage while Mark stood gaping at her in the bathroom doorway. The woman's husband didn't seem to notice; he was too preoccupied examining the grout in the shower stall.

A few minutes later, as Mark led them back down the stairs, he noticed that the pianist had abandoned Joplin in favor of plucking out random sour notes on the keyboard. It was as if the piano player had suffered a stroke while on the bench. Nonetheless, the guests still cheered on the abysmal playing.

Exhausted, Mark looked around the kitchen for Lisa, but could not find her. It seemed more people had showed up while he had been upstairs, which was strange because it was awfully late for new arrivals. He glanced at the wall clock above the sink and saw that the clock had ceased working at 8:39 p.m. He then glanced at his wrist before realizing he hadn't worn his wristwatch.

Someone began playing "Chopsticks" on the piano. Badly.

Mark shouted, "Lisa?" but doubted she could hear him over the cacophony of their guests, the piano, and the muddled jazz coming from the detachable iPod speakers. His head throbbed. "Excuse me, excuse me," he mumbled, cutting through the crowd. When he reached the parlor, he saw men dancing with men, women dancing with women, and a huddle of striped polo shirts standing around the piano. "Chopsticks" ended abruptly and the guests began haranguing the pianist. Mark saw the pianist try to stand, catching a glimpse of the familiar hairdo and dress, and thought, *Lisa.*

It was. She sat before the piano, several hands on her shoulders as if to hold her in place, while her hands sat now in her lap. A terrified expression was etched across her face. She did not know how to play the piano—baring, apparently, a rudimentary rendition of "Chopsticks"—and when she met Mark's eyes, he could see all the fear bottled up inside her. He reached out and she grasped his hand…but then *other* hands shoved him down onto the piano bench beside her.

"Play 'Heart and Soul,'" someone shouted.

"I want to get up," Lisa uttered very close to Mark's ear.

"Lean on my shoulder and I'll play," he told her.

After he had played "Heart and Soul" twice, he grasped Lisa's hand and tugged her up off the bench. Hands tried to shove them back down but Mark swatted them away as he dragged Lisa toward the kitchen. There were so many people in the parlor now it was becoming difficult to breathe.

"I'm so tired," Lisa said. "I don't think a single person has gone home yet."

"They just—" He was about to say *keep coming* when the patio door swooshed open again and another bright-eyed, pleasant-smelling couple appeared in the doorway.

"Hello!" boomed the man.

"So *nice* to finally meet you both!" cried the woman.

Lisa smiled at them wearily. Mark paused to shake their hands. To his surprise, the woman leaned in and kissed him on the corner of his mouth. The kiss lasted longer than it should have, and although it was dry and unobtrusive, she exhaled into his nostrils before pulling away. It was like tasting her breath. Instantaneously, Mark felt an erection threaten the front of his pants.

"I'd love to see the upstairs," the woman said to him, her stare hanging between them like cabling.

"In just a minute," he said, excusing himself, and dragging Lisa into the kitchen.

"Do you mind if we put on another pot of coffee, Lisa, dear?" said Betsy, coming up and breathing in Lisa's face.

"Well," Lisa said, her eyes skirting the room. "Do you think people will—"

"You're a peach!" said Betsy, then twirled away to address the coffee pot on the kitchen counter.

"I'm exhausted," Lisa moaned to Mark again. "It's got to be close to midnight."

"The clock is dead," he told her, glancing up at it again. Only now, it read 8:42 p.m. As he stared, he could see the second hand moving at nearly imperceptible increments. "Or," he amended, "it's *nearly* dead."

"Excuse me," Lisa said to Betsy. She pointed to the woman's sparkly gold wristwatch. "What time do you have?"

"Oh!" Betsy cooed. "Don't tell me you two are bushed already!" The woman glanced at her wristwatch. "Why, it's not even nine yet!"

Lisa said, "I'm sorry—did you just say it's not even *nine* yet? Nine o'clock?"

"This coffee smells so *good*," Betsy said with a wink, then turned back to the coffee pot. She began shoveling spoonfuls of coffee into the percolator.

From the parlor, someone shouted Mark's name. When Mark turned, he saw a man he did not know waving him into the room. "I hear you're a regular Liberace!"

Mark just shook his head, a drawn expression on his face.

A woman in a dark blue beret appeared in front of Mark and Lisa and said, "I think you were a bit premature putting the food away. Do you mind if I break it back out? The Wilsons haven't even shown up yet, and they'll be ravenous!"

Lisa just blinked at the woman dumbly.

"Have at it," Mark interjected, then dragged Lisa out into the hallway.

Yet the hallway was cluttered with people, too. Hands extended to shake theirs, to pat their backs, to congratulate them and welcome them to the neighborhood. Again, those invisible fingers gave Mark's abdomen a pinch. This time he whirled around to address the culprit...but found himself staring at a wall of tightly-packed people, any of whom could have been the violator.

Claustrophobia tightening around his neck, he pulled Lisa toward the staircase. Together, they bounded up the stairs to the second floor...yet froze at the top of the stairs as they saw the queue of people standing in the upstairs hallway. Wide eyes peered into the bedrooms. People murmured as they examined the bathrooms, the hall closets. A man in a tweed sports coat and a corduroy necktie stood before one open closet door, one of their bath towels in his hands. As Mark and Lisa watched, the man brought the towel to his nose and sniffed it.

"Enough," Mark called out. "It's getting late. We're going to have to ask that we at least keep the party downstairs. We'd appreciate it if—" But he cut himself off when he realized no one was listening to him.

"Mark," Lisa said, and touched his arm.

Angry, he stormed back downstairs—

"Mark!"

—and shoved through the guests in the hallway on his way to the front door. It took nearly a full minute for him to reach the door, grasp the knob, yank it open.

A man and a woman stood on the stoop, a platter of cookies in the woman's hands. They both smiled warmly at Mark, their teeth big and bright. Mark could see lipstick on some of the woman's teeth.

"Ah," said the man. "You must be Mark Schoenfield. Welcome to the neighborhood, old sailor."

Hands grabbed Mark around the forearms. Fingers snatched at his shirt and the legs of his pants. He craned his neck around to see the ghoulishly smiling faces of the men from the parlor breathing down his neck.

"You're quite the virtuoso," said Bob O'Leary. There was spinach dip stuck in his teeth. "Come play us that horror theme again, will you?"

Mark yanked one of his arms free.

"Aw, come on, now," Bob said, frowning playfully. "Don't be a spoilsport." Bob checked his wristwatch. "It's early yet."

Lisa appeared on the stairwell. Mark met her eyes. She opened her mouth to say something to him, but was immediately approached by the young couple who had come through the patio door and requested a tour of the house. Mark saw Lisa shake her head. Nonetheless, the couple advanced on her, ascending the stairs. Lisa slowly backed away from them, moving up the stairs herself. She glanced one last time at Mark before her head disappeared beyond the ceiling. He watched her legs move backward up the stairs as the couple continued to advance on her.

Bob O'Leary and some of the other men dragged him through the kitchen toward the parlor.

"Seriously," Mark said, trying to shrug them all off. "I'm in no mood to play. It's late. Everyone needs to go home now."

"Coffee's on!" Betsy trilled from the counter. A wave of people flowed toward her.

"Late?" Bob O'Leary said. Then he pointed to the clock above the kitchen sink. "What's the matter with you, Mark?"

The clock read 8:50 p.m.

"That clock is wrong," Mark said. He gripped the countertop and kicked at some of the more aggressive hands. They let him go. "It's late," he said, his breath coming in labored gasps now. "That clock is wrong."

Bob O'Leary's face seemed to crease down the middle with frustration and, Mark thought, something akin to anger, too. He thrust his wristwatch in Mark's face. Mark stared at the digital numbers. "Is *my* watch wrong?" Bob O'Leary wanted to know. "Is it, Mark?"

Bob O'Leary's watch read 8:50 p.m. As Mark stared at it, he saw the dual numbers indicating the seconds hang on 32. As he watched, the seconds did not change...did not change...did not change...until *finally* the 2 turned into a 3. It took what felt like a full minute for one second to tick by.

Mark shook his head.

"So," Bob O'Leary started up again, that cheerful smile back in place, "how about regaling us with some tickling of the ivories?"

"Oh, yes!" chirped a woman in a houndstooth scarf. "That would be lovely!"

The hands returned, gripping him high up on the forearms, at the wrists, around the waist. Someone clenched him hard high on the thigh. Bob O'Leary winked at him...then reached down and tweaked Mark's penis through the front of his pants.

Upstairs, something heavy tipped over and smashed to the floor. A moment later, someone cranked the volume on the iPod.

"No!" Mark shouted as his guests dragged him toward the parlor and the piano. "No! Leave me alone! Let me go!"

"It's so early, Mark," Bob O'Leary said.

"We've got all the time in the world," said another man.

"All the time in the world," the woman in the houndstooth scarf echoed.

Mark Schoenfield screamed.

"Party pooper," Bob O'Leary said, laughing.

THE TIDE KING

Jen Michalski *is the author of the novels* The Tide King *(Black Lawrence Press, 2013),* The Summer She Was Under Water *(Queens Ferry Press, 2016), two collections of fiction, and a couplet of novellas called* Could You Be With Her Now *(Dzanc Books, 2013). She hosts the Starts Here! reading series and lives in Baltimore. She earned her M.S. in Professional Writing from Towson University in 1999.*

1942

It was almost time to go. His mother, Safine Polensky, would see him out the door but not to the train station. She would not watch him leave on the train, his face framed in the window, his garrison cap covering his newly shorn head. She would see him to the door, where he could go to work, to school, to the store, and in the corresponding memory of her mind, he would return.

She opened the lock of the rose-carved jewelry box on the kitchen table with a butter knife, the key orphaned in Poland somewhere. He wondered whether she would produce a pocket watch, a folding knife, his father's or his uncle's, that he could fondle while trying to sleep on the hard earth, dirt full of blood and insides, exposed black tree roots cradling his head like witch fingers.

He opened his hand, waiting. She pulled out an envelope, old and brown, and the dark, furry object he regarded. A mouse carcass. A hard moldy bread.

"Burnette saxifrage." She put the crumbly mound in his palm. "Most powerful herb. I save it until now."

He glanced at the leaves and roots spread over his palm, dried like a fossilized bird. His lips tightened. His whole life to that point a stew of herbs, chalky and bitter and syrupy in his teas, his soups, rubbed onto his knees and elbows after school. Safine had brought them from the homeland, Reszel, Poland—stories of baba yagas and herbs and the magic of her youth. He may have believed once, been scared, as a child. He put it back in the envelope, more fragile than the herb.

"You take this." She grabbed his palm, her knuckles blue and bulbous. "Eternal life. You take it when you are about to die. You will live. This is the only one. You understand?"

He nodded, pushing it into the far pocket of his duffel bag, where he was certain to forget about it. Herbs had not saved his father from pains. They had not spared his mother's hands, curled and broken, her lungs, factory black. How would they save his head from being half blown off, his guts from being hung like spaghetti on someone's bayonet? He hugged her. She smelled like garlic and dust. Then he, Stanley Polensky, walked to the Baltimore station, got on the train, and went to war.

1943

They carried what they could carry. Most men carried two pairs of socks in their helmets, K-rations in their pockets, their letters and cigarettes in their vests. That queer little private, Stanley Polensky, also carried a book, and it was not the Bible.

"Polensky, throw that thing away." With the nose of his carbine, Calvin Johnson, also a private, poked him in the small of his back, where a children's book, Tom Swift and His Planet Stone, was tucked in his pants, under his shirt. "No wonder you can't get any."

"At least I can read." Polensky flipped him the bird over his shoulder. They were in a line, two men across, stretching for miles from Cerami on their way to Troina. Stanley Polensky was a boy who, back in Ohio, Johnson would have given the full order to. He would have nailed him with a football where he sat in the bleachers, reading a book. He would have spitballed him from the back of class or given him a wedgie in the locker room after track. Polensky had cried in his bunk at night for their first week at Fort Benning, wrote long letters to his mother the way others wrote to their girls.

Now, Johnson stared at his slight, curved back all day, the sun hotter than fire. On narrow trails in the hills, they pulled themselves up with ropes and cleats through passes that only they and their mules—the dumbest, smelliest articles of military equipment ever used to transport supplies—could navigate, driving back enemy strongholds at Niscemi, Ponte Olivo Airport, Mazzarino, Barrafranca, Villarosa, Enna, Alimena, Bompietro, Petralia, Gangi, Sperlinga, Nicosia, Mistretta, Cerami, and Gagliano. It would seem so easy if not so many men died, if Johnson was not walking on an ankle he'd jammed on a hill that had swollen to the size of a softball. And yet their toughest fighting was still to come, at Troina, with Germans shooting at them from the mountains in every direction.

But not today. Today there was sky and food and the Germans to the east of them.

"You want these?" Polensky tossed the hard candies from his K rations over to Johnson. Every day, they had scrambled eggs and ham, biscuits, coffee, and four cigarettes for breakfast; cheese, biscuits, hard candy, and cigarettes for lunch; and a ham and veal loaf, biscuits, hard candies, and cigarettes for dinner.

"I thought a nancy boy like you liked a little candy now and then." Johnson stuffed them in his mouth, pushing them into his cheeks like a squirrel.

"I haven't brushed my teeth in months." Stanley shook his head. "I'm afraid I'm going to lose them all."

"Well, I'll tell you what." Johnson lit his cigarette. "If I come across a toothbrush in my travels, I'll save it for you."

"I think you'll have better luck finding a Spanish galleon." Stanley lit his own cigarette.

"What do you know about Spanish galleons?"

"What do you want to know?"

"I don't know." Johnson closed his eyes. He had not done well in school. When he did not get a football scholarship to Ohio State, he thought he'd become a police officer, like his father. Knowing the war would help his chances, he'd enlisted the first opportunity he got. "What is it, like money or something?"

"No." Stanley drawled, smiling. "It's a ship."

"Warship?"

"And commerce, too. They sailed mostly in the 16th to 18th centuries."

"Is that what you learned in that Tom Swift book?" Johnson opened his eyes, studied Stanley lying on his back, knees swinging open and closed, smoke pluming upward between them.

"Wouldn't you like to know?" Stanley stared at the sky. His eyes broke up smiling when he looked at you, happy or sad. They squished a little, the outsides wrinkling, along with his forehead, his cheeks dimpling. Polensky was the youngest of six. Johnson had always wanted siblings. His mother had him. Another had died in the womb.

He imagined Stanley as a little brother and grimaced. But you took what you got, not what you wanted.

***

They set the pup tent over an abandoned trench that they could roll into if any funny business found its way to the camp. They laid boot to head. Stanley was a kicker. It was easier if Johnson fell asleep first.

"Read me something from your book." Johnson laid his arms across his stomach. When they'd first started the whole bloody business, in Africa, he'd seen a soldier trying to hold in his intestines after getting shot, a slippery pink worm pulsing out between his fingers.

"Read it yourself."

"I'm tired. What's it about?"

"Well, every book Tom invents something new. So this time, it's the metalanthium lamp."

"Metalanthium lamp? What the hell is that?"

"It's a device that emits these rays that can heal the sick and bring people back from the dead."

"Sounds interesting. How does it work?"

"I'm not telling you anymore. You want to find out, you have to read it yourself."

"I don't have time to read." Johnson rolled over, away from Stanley's feet. "In case you didn't notice, there's a war on. Why are you carrying a children's book, anyway?"

"My mother bought it for me when I was a boy."

"Couldn't you have brought something more useful?"

But Stanley had fallen asleep, his snoring choked with hot, dusty mountain air. The sound reminded Johnson of the clogged carburetor on a motorcycle he'd fixed up one summer in Ohio. At night, his own mind churned. The war had been hard to swallow. He did not know what he had expected, but he had not expected this. The exhaustion. The hollow fear—fear so intense it burned a hole through you and left you hollow. The walking. They walked along ridges and through valleys for miles and miles, up and up on roads that lead to little towns full of rock and cement houses in which lived Italians with gaunt, piercing eyes who begged for candy or sugar and cigarettes and mostly had nothing because the Germans had taken everything.

The Italian women were attractive. Sometimes he would look at them as they took his chocolate rations, their long olive necks the soft fruits of their lips, and he wanted to lay with one on the ground. Not anything sexual, although he always thought of that. He wanted to lay on the ground with one to feel her heart through her chest with his fingers, the pulse of a vein on her neck, the soft skin on the underside of her arm, to remember what it felt like, the warmth of living skin, the soft quiet of humanity in measured breaths. The skin on the dead looked like rubber, and he did not understand the difference, the living, the dead. So many had died, men in little piles, only boys, really, their limbs thrown about like tire irons, hoses, their mouths open where something had taken flight. If they could all only go on living, with quiet pulses in their necks, wrists, little bird chirps. If no one had to die, except the very old.

Sometimes it got so bad, the need to touch, he wanted to hold Stanley. He thought of waking him up and asking for the book, to take his mind off things. But he was too tired to even open his mouth. He thought of Spanish galleons instead. For some reason he imagined that they were gold like coins and flew across the ocean. But for one to take you home, you would have to die.

Johnson guessed that was fair.

1944

They were on a warship stationed in the Isle of Wight. The bunkroom was still, the usual snores, jacking off replaced by the quiet of men's eyes blinking in the dark. Before they slipped into the sheets, they had made amends with their girlfriends, their parents, with God. When they finally stepped off the landing craft the next morning onto Omaha Beach, the First Division's fate would be clear, but they would not take any chances tonight. Stanley opened the envelope lying on his chest and felt the dry fibers of the herb in the lines of his palm, which were licked with sweat. His mother had sent him care packages at Fort Benning, North Africa, and Italy—knitted socks and dollar bills wrapped in cheese cloth, a few words written carefully on lined notepaper. But she never mentioned the herb. Perhaps it was bad luck to discuss it. He had forgotten about it completely until he sewed a torn pocket on his backpack that afternoon and discovered it pushed deep within. A bit of luck, he figured. That night, he laid it on the pillow next to him. His eyes blinked; the dark sleep, dreamless, weighed them closed.

"Wake up, Polensky." A hand, heavy, dry, covered his face. "Drop your cock and grab your socks."

Johnson, from Ohio. They had entered combat in North Africa, each killed their first men in the desert. They were uneasy, unlikely, friends. Johnson was tan and shiny, a farm boy who had lettered in high school before, as he explained to Stanley, a gimpy ankle kept him from getting a scholarship to college. Stanley swore he smelled like corn, although he probably smelled like Stanley and all the others—cigarettes and rotted teeth and stink.

Stanley turned in his bunk, feeling the film of sweat break from his body and release onto the sheets. His hand trailed on the pillow, feeling for the herb, but it was empty. He shot up, nearly hitting his head on the bunk above. A man stole something that wasn't hammered down, everyone knows. Veins pulsed in Stanley's neck, his biceps. But a flower? He might kill a GI before he killed a Kraut.

"Lose something?" Johnson, bent over, emerged with the saxifrage. "Your mother's corsage?"

"What time is it?" Stanley ignored him.

"Four-thirty." Johnson straightened. The doctor measured him six foot five during their physicals. Stanley had topped out eight inches shorter. "First wave 0630 to Normandy. Better shower, get that shit off your ass."

One hundred thirty thousand men. Two years ago, Stanley could not have guessed so many to have existed in their divisions, much less his hometown, or the world. One hundred thirty thousand men dragged over the English Channel to Omaha Beach in battleships, landing craft, to fight like gladiators, mongrels. There were so many ships, Stanley wondered whether they could just cross the channel by stepping from one to another.

They climbed down the rope ladders of the battleship and into the landing craft, a steel bread box, that would shuttle them to the beach. The chop was terrible. Each wave sent that morning's oatmeal into the roof of each man's mouth, and they swallowed it again. Their helmets clicked together like teeth.

But the waves were too powerful; the landing crafts could not get in close enough to the shore to let the men out. They would have to swim. One end of the craft, its gate resting just under the water; the men stood and began to wade out waist-high. The first were sighted immediately by the 352nd Infantry German Division waiting ashore. From their concrete bunkers among the dunes and perches among the cliffs, the Germans scattered those first hundred men like pins. Shells exploded water into the boat, and the remaining men inched back, pressing against the sides as bullets rattled off the floor, walls, men.

"Picking us off like fucking lemmings," Johnson said from where he and Stanley sat in the back. He stood up and began to climb the wall of the boat. "Come on Polensky, you waiting to die?"

Stanley scrambled up the wall after Johnson, the weight of his packs and rifles pulling at him like children. The water stunned him for a second, and he was confused, thinking he was at Porter's Beach as a child, the chilled water of the Chesapeake Bay grabbing through the wool of his bathing suit and squeezing his nuts, his sister Kathryn bobbing beside him.

But it was Johnson beside him, the lasso of his arm pulling Stanley away from undertow of the boat. Stanley's fatigues stuck to him like skin. He wondered whether his rifle would work wet, if the grenades attached to his belt would go off after he threw them. He crouched in the water so only his eyes, helmet, bobbed above.

They waded to the shore, the water throwing up around them as the German shells exploded underneath, bullets flicking around them like whitecaps. No matter how fast he moved, Stanley fell behind Johnson's long stride, Johnson becoming his human shield, which filled Stanley with relief and disgust. Thirty feet in, to the right of Stanley, a man's upper body rose as if being yanked from the water by an invisible hand before sinking into the sea. The men thinned out closer to shore; if by miracle one were to make it to the beach, he was fired upon from several directions, his body a dancing pile in the surf.

The water squished in his socks and his underwear, and the straps of his backpack cut against his shoulder. He thought of stupid things while in danger, like his bedding being wet that night when he unfurled it to sleep, his cigarettes gone to mush. He touched his helmet, wondering if the herb he'd stuffed there that morning was secure. Suddenly Johnson lifted his rifle, set, and ran, firing at the shore. Stanley followed, although he thought it was a waste. He wasn't even looking at the beach. He was crouched so low that the current shoveled water into his open mouth and now here was

Johnson, moving his big legs out of the water like pistons, lead flying from his rifle, a human tank forgetting it was closer to jellyfish than steel.

But Stanley followed. He moved his legs and spread out to the right of Johnson. He felt the burning in his hamstrings, the blood straining his heart, the veins in ears ready to spout like whistles. The shelling and fire screamed in his ears until it became quiet. The beach grew on each end; he could see the bunkers of the Germans beyond the dunes. Pinholes of light flicked from them; the water spit bullets around him in response. He aimed his rifle toward the holes and fired, the kick pulled him forward. He feared his skeleton, his muscles, might fall out of his body behind him. He clamped his mouth shut and felt the shells and pebbles of the surf scrape against his knees.

He had made it. He looked left for Johnson. Good fuck, the farm boy made it, too.

***

On the beach, they found a man who was not quite dead. They wanted to find a man who was dead, but they could not be picky. The man who was not quite dead was moaning and breathing thick, gurgly, lying on his stomach. Almost dead. He and Johnson rolled the body on its side and propped their rifles on its left arm. Above them, 50 yards up the beach, lay the Longues-sur-Mer battery, or the German bunkers, huge square cement structures that housed mortars and men. Artillery fire flashed from these holes and scattered the sand around them. Stanley reached for the dying man's helmet to put between the rifles, a barrier so they could peer up to shoot. A pack of cigarettes fell to the beach from it, which Johnson picked up and pocketed. Why Stanley hadn't put his own cigarettes in his helmet to keep dry, instead of the herb, he didn't know. There was no time to mull it over. They were alive, but only by luck and perhaps not for long. Around them, disembodied heads, arms, and backpacks floated in the air before gravity pulled them back to earth. Stanley coughed and shivered, peering up and sighting his rifle on one of the bunkers.

"I'll shoot and you toss the grenade," he said to Johnson over the fire. He may have screamed it, he may have thought it. Either way, no sound seemed to come from his mouth but Johnson understood, reaching toward his belt. The body flung backward at them like a flying log, taking fire. They braced against it. If the man had not been dead, he was now.

Johnson hurled the grenade. His long arm seemed to reach out and leave the grenade at the entrance to the bunker, like a gift. They ducked, felt the vibration rumble through the sand. The smoke from the grenade curled into the grey of the sky and the grey of the sky ate the smoke. It was impossible to see where anything began or ended.

Stanley felt a pull at his trousers. A tear in the side of his pants exposed flesh, blood. A bullet had grazed him, tearing a zig-zag down his leg. The Germans hidden in the cliffs around the bunkers were shooting at them. Johnson rolled to his left, stood up, and barreled for safety to a formation of rocks fifteen feet ahead. He waved Stanley on.

One of theirs, Green, was waiting there. Blood ran down his face, cleaning it of black soot on one side. Green jerked his head toward a rip in the fortified wire around the German embankments. The sand was slippery from the blood. Stanley spread his arms like a plane and continued running, his rifle flapping against his chest.

Beyond the barbed wire they waited, the men wearing the other helmets. They seemed surprised that Stanley, Johnson, and Green were there. Months of waiting at Omaha for the Allies to strike, and now they stood, unsure, like boys at a dance. Green pulled out his pistol and shot the first man he came to in the face. The man dropped, his body hitting the earth before his blood. Stanley shoved his bayonet low into a man's stomach, avoiding the ribs. Johnson held his rifle waist high and waved, spraying all those around him with bullets.

They did this for a long time. They killed men with helmets not like theirs. They stabbed them and they shot them and they lobbed grenades at them and they twisted their necks and they did this until the other men retreated. Then they smoked some of the cigarettes they'd taken earlier. Stanley knotted his handkerchiefs, wet and pink tinged from the bloodied channel water, and tied them around his leg. He watched the cloth drink up the blood until it was full, and then Johnson gave him his handkerchiefs while Green looked for the medic.

Some other men came over and smoked their own cigarettes. Everyone was dirty and smelled and shivered. Some cried. Some prayed, their mouths wide and moving. Some went through the pockets of the Germans and put watches, cigarettes, soft-edged pictures of girls into their boots and helmets. Stanley smoked his cigarette and wished he could tell his mother he was alive. Johnson stretched out his long legs as another man squatted, fanning a fire. Stanley laid his wet, torn cigarettes on the sand to dry. Most men were quiet, although some talked. Stanley wished they would shut up. It had been two years, two continents of this shit. The only way he could get through it was with silence, the air thin and yet full of salt, the beach full of dead men and yet life still lingering. His thoughts empty, body heavy.

"Come on." Johnson stood up. "We can't leave them like that."

That work, they did silently. They stacked the bodies of their men in rows like one would stack cordwood for the ships to take them to sea. Then they emptied their own backpacks, their bowels, and waited again for their orders.

***

They spent the summer moving inland toward Germany. The war will be over soon, Stanley wrote his mother. His twentieth letter. The Germans are running like cowards. He played poker with Johnson and Ennis, throwing pennies and cigarettes and girlie pictures into a German helmet they used as a pot. I hope you are well and do not worry about me. He spent one week at Netley Hospital for his leg wound. Nothing much has happened to us in Europe, except we are getting fatter. He lost twenty pounds since leaving the States. Hopefully by the time you get this, I will be on the train home. In September, they entered the Hürtgen forest.

"I would die for a ham," Johnson let his cigarette dangle as he settled in the brush. It was a game they played sometimes, what they would die for, since they might die for much less.

"I would die for a turkey sandwich," Stanley answered. Spruce and balsam trees cloaked their eyes, yielding little forest beyond a few feet. The tree limbs, low, grabbed, and the men walked with a semi-permanent stoop.

"I would die for a woman's hips. I would put myself between them and sleep like the dead." Johnson grinned, his teeth white against the green cave. Water dripped constantly. The men could never find the source of it. Sometimes it confused Stanley, and when he slept for brief periods and woke, he thought he was at his parent's house, down the hall from the leaky faucet.

"Stay here." Johnson's arm would grab for Stanley's ankle as Stanley began to push forward through the brush.

"The sink is fucking leaking," Stanley waved him off, before Johnson yanked and Stanley fell down into the bed of pine needles that covered the forest floor.

"I would die to get out of this forest," Stanley said as they ate the last of their bread and coffee. The supply lines inland were farther away, their rations fewer.

"I would die for dry socks." The mud and fog lay on them like a film. In the dark undergrowth, the men rubbed against the trees and each other like ingredients in a stew. Where were the Germans? Surely not as stupid as the Americans, Stanley thought, burrowing through the forest, their tanks and artillery and Air Force stalled by the dense formations of trees and rough terrain. The Allies were all alone.

***

Stanley peed in the snow. The cold air crept into his open pants and ran down his legs. Before he could even finish the German shelling of the tree canopy began again, and Stanley crouched and hugged the spruce in front of him without even pulling up his zipper. Around him, splinters from the trees rained down like daggers, along with hot metal. Ennis had looked like a wooden porcupine when they pulled him back behind their lines a few days before. The shrapnel in Ennis' chest had been bad, and he and Johnson, trapped in front of a patch of machine guns, pressed themselves to the snow and needles and mud for hours, Ennis between them, moaning for his mother.

Three days earlier, the First Division had discovered the Germans, hidden and waiting for the Allies to amble past the river, when their eyes were tired of the undulation of snow and trees, when their bodies were cold because, in anticipation of quick victory, the Allied brass had not thought to ship winter clothes to the front. For weeks, as the Northern chill swept in, Stanley and Johnson and the others had measured their boots against dead men's, their inseams, their chest sizes, looking to replace their wet, worn clothes with ones slightly drier, slightly cleaner. Stanley wore two shirts other than his own, each caked and itchy with medals of blood.

Stanley crawled on his hands in the red and brown snow back to the slit trench he had dug with Johnson earlier that afternoon. They had covered the opening with tree limbs and hoped it would protect them from the shrapnel and wood. Inside, they were asshole buddies, sitting back to back, or asshole to asshole, chest high in the hole, branches and snow over them as they watched for movement beyond their line.

"You all right?" Johnson asked as Stanley shivered against him. After nightfall, it became frost. The dead men stuck to the earth.

"I think I'm going to have the runs something awful."

"Well, go have them the hell out there."

"You just want me shot at."

"Just go behind that tree over there. I'll cover you."

"Fuck you."

"I'm joking. Just be quiet." Johnson's hands felt frozen to his carbine. He would give his left hand, purple and granite under his glove, for a cigarette. He felt the pressure of Polenksy's back leave his, a creeping cold between his soldier blades, as Polensky turned around in the trench and squatted, helmet under his ass.

"You know, we should have a code word, a personal one, in case one of us leaves the hole." Johnson tried to talk over Stanley's sounds. A cigarette would go a long way to blunt the smell. But smoke could be seen at night. Rot, shit, and death smelled day and night, as assessable as air.

"What's wrong with the company's password?"

"Nothing. I just thought it would be good if we had our own. So I always know it's a kraut in the burned-out house I'm about to fire into and not you."

"Jesus Lord Christ," Stanley grunted from his side of the trench.

"That's not a good one, Polensky. Too many guys already know it."

"Screw you. Christ...I ain't going to wear this again, that's for sure."

"Just clean it out with some snow. You may not need to protect that empty head of yours, but where are you going to store your socks and corsage?"

"Up your ass."

"Well, I know for sure that hasn't seen any action." Johnson aimed his rifle toward a flutter by the trees on his right. Geese? Squirrels? "How about metalanthium lamp?"

"That's your word?"

"Pretty good, huh?"

Suddenly, movement rocketed upward from the same trees. Mine? Mortar? Geese, definitely geese. The feathers and pulp floated to earth, shot by two others in the company. In response, the kraut line lit up like flashbulbs. Polensky fell into position next to Johnson, his helmet, an overturned latrine, unstrapped on his chin. Around them, the snow spit bullets, feathers from feather pillows. For a second, Johnson closed his eyes, thought he would let himself get hit. To feel the cool, light fabric of a pillow, a flat one, a hard one, a moldy one, it didn't matter. His head whipped to the right, and he thought he'd gotten his wish. But it was only Stanley, punching him with an open palm.

"Wake up, dummy," he shouted at him above the soft explosions. "What the fuck are you doing?"

"Nothing," Johnson grunted, but he realized he was smiling. He liked this Stanley. He fired off a round. "Shithead."

"Go fuck yourself," Stanley answered, firing off his own. Johnson could see he was smiling, too.

***

The brass said the Hürtgen Forest was 50 square miles. It seemed to stretch to 100, then 200, then 300, as late October became early November and late November became early December. Stanley did not understand how they could not see the Germans and yet the Germans could see them.

"They know these forests. They're stuffed in bunkers while we walk right by them," Johnson said, coughing. Johnson had developed a cough-snore-shiver in his sleep. Perhaps Stanley could boil the herb for tea, soothe Johnson's deathly rattle. I still have the root, Stanley wrote to his mother. Although I suspect I will have no reason to use it. You never even told me how. Should I put it under my lip, in a wound, perhaps? His right foot smelled. There was no time to unlace the boot and find out whether his toes had rotted. We are warm and fat and happy. Save me some Chinina.

"Duck blood soup," Johnson laughed later, when Stanley described Christmas dinner at home. "You eat everything, don't you, Pole? Makes me want to come to your house to dinner after the war."

"Right now, I would eat anything," Stanley shivered. He shivered when he was awake and he shivered when he was dreaming. His breath was staccatoed with shivers. He shivered when he peed and he shivered when he shat and he shivered when he shivered. Stanley would eat his shivers, if he could, but they would probably give him diarrhea, he thought, like everything else.

***

They were still in the Hürtgen Forest, pissed as hell about it. Stanley and Johnson had taken turns moving out ahead, little by little, looking for mines and trying to clear brush for a path out. The visibility was ten feet, at best, and the soldier, with his back to Stanley, appeared from the foliage like a mirage. It had to be one of their men, so close by. Stanley tapped him on the shoulder just as he realized the man looked wrong, the uniform, the helmet. As the man turned, Stanley pulled out his revolver and plugged him in the right cheek. The man fell, the wound cratering inward in his face like a black hole before bubbling up, blood oozing on the smooth, unshaven skin.

He was a boy. Stanley wondered if he was lost. His eyelids flickered, and Stanley wondered whether he should touch them, hold his hand. He kicked away the boy's rifle. The boy's fingers opened like petals. Stanley touched the boy's forehead with his left hand, his right cocked on his pistol, near his hip.

"Mutter," the boy said, a whisper wet with blood. When he reached up toward Stanley, Stanley shot him. The arm fell back toward the body. Stanley shivered. He shivered in his heart and his throat and the tears from his eyes warmed his face until it grew cold and sticky and he shivered again. He thought to eat his mother's herb, to protect himself. It could not hurt. When one no longer believed in anything, he considered, all things could possess equal power.

"You all right?" Johnson appeared from the brush, as Stanley groped in his helmet, feeling for the crumbled flowers. He put a hand on Stanley's shoulder. His grip was gentle, as if handling crystal, unlike his usual vice of fingers that dug right into Stanley's collarbone.

"Yeah." Stanley put his helmet back on quickly without retrieving it and rolled the boy over, face down, in the snow.

***

They walked in a diamond formation: Stanley walked in the back, Johnson in the front, one man, red-haired, was to their left, another, blond-haired, to their right. Stanley didn't know their names. It seemed a waste to learn them. Wood and shrapnel fell from the sky, mixed with snow, hitting the ground in hisses. The trees burned standing still. Stanley listened to the fire eating the wood, the snap of twigs and branches as they broke free of the parent trunks and fell down to the forest. Smoke poured from the nooks and crannies of the burning bark, and men were forced to crawl. On the ground, the red-haired man, in front, would tap the top of his helmet and point in the direction of movement, and they all would crouch and fill that direction with fire, grenades. But then the blond man on the right threw a grenade that hit a tree and bounced back toward them, and they dove leftward and rolled down a small hill.

"I would die for a stick of gum." Johnson entangled himself from Stanley. The smoke cleared, briefly, and the hard marble of sun blinked through the treetops.

"This might be your lucky day." Stanley nodded. Before them, a formation of rock appeared in the trees with a low opening, two by eight feet. A bunker. The red-haired man stood off to the side of it. He tossed in a grenade as they turned, covered their ears. Then they waited for the smoke to clear before joining him at the hole.

Stanley was the shortest, so he got on his knees and crawled in. He imagined a speckling of dead pale boys, boys with smooth faces and darting eyes, but it was empty with black. He tapped the inner mouth of the cave to make sure it was still secure. Then he pointed his thumb up, and the others joined him.

"Now this is living," red hair said in the darkness. He lit a cigarette and stretched. "We stay here until the war ends, okay?"

"At least for a nap," Stanley agreed, pulling his blanket out of his backpack. "We'll take turns on watch."

They slept on ground that wasn't wet and in corners that weren't windy. They slept with their helmets off, their boots unlaced, oblivious to the shelling outside. When they woke, their stomachs were relaxed, growling. They wondered how to get back behind the line for rations, wondered where they were.

"I say we stay in the hole," the red-haired man said.

"Yeah, and when one of our own boys throws another grenade in here, then what?" the blond said, tightening his laces. They were broken and did not go all the way up the boot.

"That's why we take turns on watch." The red-haired man shook his head.

"And when our whole company leaves us behind?" Johnson loaded his rifle. "We'll starve to death in the woods."

"Moving thirty feet a day?" red-haired man sneered. "Not fucking likely we get left behind."

"My orders were to take the forest," Johnson craned his head out of the hole. "I don't know about yours."

Their mood was sour. They decided to follow the ravine that led from the bunker.

"All aboard the Kraut trail," Johnson laughed. "Think they'll shell us here?"

"I say we're mighty close to something." Stanley lit a cigarette. "Think we're near the West Wall?"

"By God, we should be so lucky," the blond man said. "Then we can shoot the hell out of them and go home."

Stanley could not picture home. His mother's face appeared vaguely, the smell of her, the sound of her. The hardware store where he worked on Eastern Avenue. His school, Baltimore Polytechnic. He could not be sure whether any of those things had happened or whether they were a dream. Whether he had always been at war and would always be. They walked along the ravine for hours. Sometimes they would come across a body of a German, always picked clean. One body was missing its fillings, the mouth open and exposing bloody stumps of gumline.

"We need to find some Krauts so we can take their braut," the blond man said.

"I'd even eat the fucking Krauts," the red-haired man said. "Maybe we should go back and find our men."

"Maybe you're right," Stanley said. "Even if we find the Germans, they'll probably outnumber us."

"Our men are probably ahead of us," Johnson said, his head nodding forward. "That's why we're seeing so many dead. I told you we got left behind."

"Not likely," the red-haired man said. "I'm going back. The whole month, I ain't seen nobody get ahead of me. If there's somebody ahead of us, it's a different division. Which I'm more than happy for. Let them take some shots."

"I'm with him." The blond turned in the slit trench. "Come on, safety in numbers." Red gripped his rifle. "Let's go back."

"What say you?" Johnson looked at Stanley. Johnson was the leader, but Stanley wanted to find their squadron, food.

"Let's go back." Stanley didn't look at Johnson.

"The Pole has decided," Johnson said, spitting in the trench, kicking at the snow-dirt with his shoe. "Let's go."

***

They turned around and followed the slit trench back to the bunker. Then they climbed up the slope they had fallen down earlier.

"Let's sweep out and move forward," Stanley said. Stanley moved in front, Johnson in the back. The shelling shook and shredded the tree canopy above them, branches falling like swooping vultures, pelting their shoulders and arms, leaving welts. The raining wood and shells filled the air with the sound of sanding metal, and Stanley could not hear anyone, only see their jaws moving, their eyes flicking back and forth as they scanned the area for mines, for Germans, for secure ground in front of them. Stanley wished they had stayed in the bunker. He glimpsed a man running through the trees, white and red cross armband. A medic. They knew how to get back to the line. All they needed to do was follow him. Stanley motioned to the men and ran toward the figure.

He had not gotten far when the ground swelled behind him like a wave, sweeping him off his feet. A shell. His body hit the dirt at angles—elbow, knees, ankles—before rolling. When he stopped, he felt for his legs, moved them, and stood up, crouched over.

"Johnson?" he called back. The area from where he had been thrown was peppered with wood and metal. Blackened bark. Gray and red snow. Johnson's helmet.

He followed the trail to Johnson, what was left of him. Blood spread from the left side of Johnson's groin, his left leg scattered around him, bone broken and carved like scrimshaw and strewn with strips of muscle and skin. Johnson shivered, coughed, and looked lazily up at Stanley, drunk with shock. Stanley called for the medic. The blond man staggered up and then off, shouting for help. Stanley tore a strip of cloth from Johnson's backpack and made a tourniquet. Johnson's big long face caved in from his cheeks to his chin. His eyes fluttered.

"Johnson." Stanley shook him. But Johnson was going. Stanley took off his helmet and scooped the herb out of the lining. He opened Johnson's mouth and pushed it in.

But Johnson didn't chew. Stanley opened Johnson's mouth and pulled a third of it between Johnson's gums and teeth. He picked off another piece and put in the red, beating hole that was once Johnson's hip, leg. Then he moved Johnson's jaw with his own hands, pushing Johnson's tongue aside, grinding the herb with Johnson's teeth. Johnson's mouth was dry as cotton, and the herb coated the soft pink insides. Stanley stuck his finger in Johnson's mouth and pushed the flakes, the unchewed pieces, into Johnson's throat. Johnson gagged, sitting up and coughing, hands at his neck. The green-brown flakes flew out, covering Stanley's face and shirt. Stanley wrapped his arms under Johnson's chest and jerked upward. Stanley jerked and Johnson coughed and the herb chunk flew into the snow.

"Medic." The man dropped his kit beside Stanley. Stanley moved back and caught sight of the spat-out herb. It glowed in the detritus, unearthly. Stanley's heart jumped. He reached for the glowing orange saxifrage. The medic turned, shook his head, frowned.

Johnson was dead. The medic tagged him, took one of his dog tags, and scrambled back in the forest. It seemed wrong to leave Johnson like this, any of them like this. Maybe Stanley wouldn't fight anymore, stay here with Johnson, work the herb into his wounds, down his throat. He could stick his knife into Johnson's chest and massage it into his heart.

The trees shook around him. Men shouted in the distance, the trill of bullets, explosions. Small fires baked in pockets of black trees. When another shell landed to the left of Stanley, he could feel the warmth of it on his leg. He did what he later imagined any other person would do. He ran.

NEWPORT

*Jill **Morrow** has enjoyed a broad spectrum of careers including practicing law and singing with local bands. She holds a bachelor's degree in history from Towson University and a J.D. from the University of Baltimore School of Law. Jill currently lives outside Baltimore, Maryland, but she has a special place in her heart for Maine, Boston, and Chicago, not always in that order. You can visit her at www.jillmorrow.net. What follows is the first chapter of her novel* Newport, *which takes place in 1921 after World War I. Prohibition is in full swing and the Great Depression is still years away. Attorney Adriane de La Noye returns to the city of his misspent youth to revise the will of a well-heeled client, only to to become entangled in a world of séances and romantic drama..*

The lighthouse on the shore flashed its beacon in time with each rolling heave of Jim Reid's stomach. His knuckles whitened around the metal railing of the boat as he leaned forward, willing the wicked water to swallow him up whole and end his misery now. "Holy Mother of God," he groaned.

"Good grief, Mr. Reid. We're crossing Narragansett Bay, not the high seas." Adrian de la Noye's words cut through the nighttime dimness of the ferry deck. Disembodied in the shadows, his silken tone carried the same authority it did when summing up a complicated case before a Boston jury.

For at least the tenth time since they'd boarded Adrian's Pierce-Arrow Town Car earlier that day, Jim swore beneath his breath at his own weakness—soft Irish words that he remembered from childhood but could no longer translate.

"Sorry to be such a wet blanket," he said. "I'm doing the best I can."

There was a pause as Adrian considered. "Of course you are," he said. "You always do, my boy. You always do."

The smell of phosphorous hung on the air as a match arced through the darkness toward the cigarette in Adrian's mouth. Illuminated briefly by the flame, his chiseled features appeared almost otherworldly, his dark hair and eyes conjuring images more akin to pirates and gypsies than to prosperous middle age. Jim would have traded even his fresh new Harvard Law sheepskin for some of that smooth coolness. It wasn't likely he'd ever attain it without some sort of miracle. He was tall and lanky, with fair skin that blushed at the slightest provocation and a sandy-colored cowlick that doomed him to be viewed more boyish than manly by nearly every female who crossed his path.

"Here." Adrian handed him the cigarette. "It will settle your stomach."

Grateful, Jim pulled in a deep drag. Even he could manage some degree of cleverness with a cigarette resting lightly between his fingers. Sometimes smoking felt like the most valuable lesson he'd learned in school. The godawful queasiness began to subside.

Adrian lit a cigarette for himself and leaned his elbow casually against the ferry's railing. The lighthouse receded off to the left, leaving the gentle glow of the stars to wash across the deck. Jim pushed his wire-rimmed glasses farther up his nose and let out a long, relieved sigh.

The smoldering tip of Adrian's cigarette picked up glints in his gold tie pin, made the fine amethyst stone at its center glitter. Jim winced as he remembered one more thing he had to do: search the floor of the Town Car for his own tie pin, which he'd flung there in annoyance after stabbing himself one time too many that day.

"We've almost reached Aquidneck Island," Adrian said. "Newport is a short drive from the quay. I'll need only a moment to send Constance a telegram. She'll want to know we've arrived safely."

"Do you think we'll find any place open?"

Adrian shrugged. "We'll manage something."

For as long as Jim had known Adrian de la Noye—and that was practically all of his twenty-five years—the man had never seemed ruffled or out of place. Such ease was to be expected in the sanctified halls of Andover and Harvard, which Jim had attended on Adrian's dime. Adrian had been born to fit into places like that, and he called both institutions alma mater. As far as Jim was concerned, each school could consider itself darn lucky. What surprised him more was that Adrian was equally at home in the Reid family's noisy South Boston row house, where a seemingly endless number of Jim's siblings, nieces, and nephews had tumbled across Mr. de la Noye's well-dressed knees throughout the years. For all his accomplishments, Adrian seemed to require little more than the comfortable life he shared with his wife, Constance, and their two children back in Brookline.

Jim glumly flicked his ashes into the bay. He himself never quite fit anywhere. Over-educated in his boyhood neighborhood, but not of the usual social class found at Harvard, he was a perennial fish out of water, getting by through the sheer power of his mind.

"Ah." A husky female voice behind Jim's shoulder startled him. "Real men smoking real ciggies. Please, darlings, tell me those are Fatimas."

Adrian reached into his coat pocket as both men turned to face the woman behind them. "They are. May I offer you one?"

"I thought you'd never ask."

The woman was of average height, dressed in a light frock well suited to a sweet young thing. She needn't have bothered. The way she stroked Adrian's hand as he lit her cigarette marked her as anything but sweet, and it was obvious she hadn't been young in years. The stylish dropped waist of her dress could not conceal a matronly thickening about her middle, and beneath her gay cloche and bobbed fair hair, her jawline began to sag.

She plucked the match from Adrian's fingers and tossed it into the water. Then, insinuating herself snugly between the two men, she leaned back against the ferry's rail and dragged nicotine deep into her lungs. The exhaled smoke wafted into the air, borne on vapors of alcohol. The woman swayed, evidence more of her own intoxication than of the ferry's movement. Adrian steadied her before she could tumble into his arms and took a discreet step to his left. Jim didn't bother to move at all. It didn't matter that the woman's arm had just brushed his wrist. He could drop his trousers and jump up and down on the deck were he so inclined; he was sure she'd never notice.

"I can't resist Fatimas...or the men who smoke them," the woman said. "Virginia tobacco can't hold a candle to the virility...of a true Turkish blend."

Adrian flashed a polite smile. "Indeed," he said.

It was the same everywhere they went. Whether the female was a doll or a chunk of lead, she always chose Adrian. Jim sighed, wondering what it would be like to leave every woman in your wake weak-kneed with desire. Granted, this one wasn't worth it. But how was it that Adrian was never tempted to slip? Given the opportunity, Jim would have been delighted to slip nearly every time.

"The name is Chloe," the woman said. "Lady Chloe Chapman Dinwoodie to the rest of the world, but you may now consider yourself my friends. Excuse me." She bent down, lifted the hem of her dress, and withdrew a contraband flask from the garter tied around her pudgy leg. "Drinkie?"

"No, thank you," Adrian said.

Recognition hit Jim like a smack to the side of the head. "Say you're..."

Adrian corked his flowing words with one veiled glance. "Mr. Reid has perhaps heard of your father," he said. "Bennett Chapman's contributions to the textiles industry are very well known."

Chloe's expression soured. "Damn the old coot. I'm missing a weekend of parties in New York to ossify in Newport because of him." She threw her head back and took a long swig from the flask. Adrian met Jim's gaze over the swallowing motion of her throat.

"Yes, sir," Chloe Dinwoodie said, coming up for air. "Let's drink to good old Pop and his contributions to the textiles industry."

"His success is admirable," Adrian said mildly.

"Then let's drink to good old Pop and his contributions to Chloe's lifestyle." She again extended the flask in a silent invitation. Adrian shook his head. "Let's drink to the family manses in Boston, New York, London, and Newport," she continued. "And let's not forget how that money bought me a titled husband, too. A shame the fool's a fairy, but he does come with benefits."

She tossed her half-smoked Fatima over the ferry railing. Adrian wordlessly extended another.

"You're a dear man." Chloe waited as he lit a match, then pulled his hand closer to guide the flame toward the cigarette now clamped between her bright red lips.

Adrian did not move away this time. Instead he bathed her in one of those intimate gazes Jim recognized from his mentor's arsenal of cross-examination techniques.

"Of course you'd rather be elsewhere," Adrian said. "Newport certainly isn't the jewel she used to be. What coaxed you away from the glitter of New York?"

Chloe's fingers tightened around his wrist. "Oh, only dire circumstances could do that, I assure you. My father wants to change his will."

Jim's face burned with the flood of a hot red flush. Words bubbled to his lips.

Adrian intercepted them with the graceful stealth of a panther. "I assume the change is not to your advantage," he murmured.

Chloe's round-eyed stare resembled a mesmerized trance. "Advantage? It's a disaster! Nicholas and I—Nicky's my brother—will be flat out of luck if he goes through with it. Right now we stand to get everything when my father kicks the bucket...meets his Maker... you know. But now Pop wants to marry this...gold digger."

"Ah. There's a woman involved."

"Isn't there always? Anyway, that's why Pop wants to change his will. And if he goes through with it, Nicky and I get a yearly stipend apiece and that's it."

"I see your difficulty," Adrian said. "But how can you stop him?"

Chloe dropped her voice to a confidential whisper. "Pop's got his Boston prig of a lawyer coming up to draft the new will tomorrow. Nicky says that if we can prove our father is nuts, the will must legally stand as is. Nicky's a dull stick, but he's smart about things like this."

Adrian's voice dropped as well. "Can you prove that your father is incompetent?"

"Oh, yes." Chloe stepped forward until only an inch separated the lace of her collar from Adrian de la Noye's well-tailored vest. "With what's been going on around his place lately? Oh, absolutely yes. You know, I don't believe you've told me your name."

Jim could almost see the noxious alcohol fumes snaking their way up Adrian's nostrils. Adrian abhorred inebriation, deemed it sloppy and unnecessary. It probably required a supreme act of will for him to stand still, smiling blandly as the Lady Chloe Chapman Dinwoodie walked her fingernails up his chest.

A snicker worked its way through Jim's nose. He quickly turned away, disguising his laughter with an unconvincing sneeze. This tendency to lose his composure at the mere thought of the absurd was yet another bad habit he needed to conquer.

A sudden movement on the deck stopped his sniggering flat. Farther down the rail, a figure crouched, half hidden by a weathered box of life preservers. Startled, Jim leaned forward. The figure jumped under his scrutiny and flattened itself against the box as if trying to disappear. It was too late; Jim had seen plenty. He identified the cap and knickers of a young boy, noted that the figure was small and slight. But, most important, he knew without a doubt that for some reason, this boy had been listening intently to every word.

"Hey!" Jim lunged toward the life preservers, but the boy was faster. The small figure skittered across the deck and out of sight.

"May I offer assistance, Mr. Reid?" Adrian appeared instantly at his side.

Jim's shoulders sagged as he blinked at the empty space before him. "I'll tell you later, when there's no fear of ears. It's probably nothing; I'm just a little jumpy."

"Any particular reason?" Adrian threw a glance toward Lady Dinwoodie, who now slumped against the ferry rail like a deflated balloon, lost in an inebriated haze.

Jim shook his head, hard. "This whole trip reeks, that's all."

"In what way?"

"I don't know. It just feels...off. Taking this trip to the old man's summer cottage in the first place—"

"Mr. Chapman has been a valued client of our firm for many years."

"—then running across his daughter like this..."

"An admittedly awkward coincidence, although I found her comments most enlightening."

"You had no idea that Bennett Chapman's will might be contested?"

"Not an inkling. Naturally, we'll re-adjust our plans accordingly. We'll stay in town tonight and visit Liriodendron tomorrow. That will give Lady Dinwoodie an opportunity to compose herself."

Jim removed his spectacles to massage the crease in his brow. "You don't think she'll remember us the second we knock on Liriodendron's door?"

They turned as one toward Chloe Chapman Dinwoodie, but she had tottered away, presumably in search of new prey.

A corner of Adrian's mouth turned up. "Given the amount of bootleg she's consumed, Chloe Dinwoodie will be fortunate if she remembers how she arrived at Liriodendron in the first place. I suspect we'll register as nothing more than a bad dream. Suppose we wait in the car. That will save us from meeting the charming Lady again."

With a resigned sigh, Jim followed his mentor to the auto. He was no longer particularly connected to his Irish past, no more so than any other first generation American born and raised in South Boston. Why was it, then, that he could now hear the lilting voice of his departed Granny Cullen, who'd always claimed that the blood of ancient Celtic soothsayers warmed her veins? He'd grown up with her predictions and warnings, and this one trumpeted as loudly as any of them: "Little good ever comes of mixing where you aren't wanted."

Despite Bennett Chapman's invitation, it was clear that most of Liriodendron's occupants would be more than happy to slam the front door in Adrian de la Noye's face.

"Adrian..." Jim stopped still on the deck.

Adrian turned toward him, one eyebrow raised in inquiry.

Jim hesitated. He was indebted to Adrian's kindness, could never have come this far without his patronage. But it was more than that: dashing, sure-footed Adrian de la Noye was everything he wanted to be. Summoning superstitions from the old country would only further emphasize the differences between them.

"Never mind," Jim said slowly. "I'm tired, that's all."

"All the better reason for a good night's sleep before we visit Liriodendron. I'll need that sharp mind of yours, Mr. Reid. I've grown to depend on it."

Jim followed along in silence, trying to forget that his granny's predictions had seldom been wrong.

2100

Andrew Payton writes fiction, poetry, and nonfiction, and has had his work published in Meridian, Greensboro Review, Masters Review, The Rumpus, South Dakota Review, Southern Humanities Review, Third Coast *and* Notre Dame Review, *among other journals and magazines. His poem "Bad May" won the 2013 James Hearst Poetry Prize at North American Review, his story "Potomac" received a finalist prize in* The Chicago Tribune*'s 2014 Nelson Algren Award for short fiction, and his essay "Family Medicine" was a Notable Essay in* Best American Essays 2013. *He was a 2013 fellow at the Aspen Summer Words Writing Retreat, a finalist for the 2014 Fiction Fellowships at the Wisconsin Institute of Creative Writing, and a 2014-15 recipient of the J. William Fulbright fellowship to the Slovak Republic. Payton originally graduated from Towson University in 2008 with a B.A. in English and Electronic Media and Film, and later also became a graduate of the M.F.A. Program in Creative Writing and Environment at Iowa State University.*

When his teacher projected a map on the screen she sometimes pulled over the chalkboard, Arthur Leonard learned that his neighborhood would one day be underwater.

Arthur raised his hand, asked, "When?"

"Six and a half feet by 2100," the teacher said.

"How far away is that?" he asked.

"I won't be alive," she said. "But you all might."

Since seeing the maps, in the time between the school bus dropping him off and his mother coming home from the restaurant, Arthur has been walking the neighborhood with chalk and ruler. He picks his favorite buildings—the church that paid him five dollars an hour to scrape and paint the shingles last summer break, the old theatre where seat cushions spray stuffing and chandeliers dangle cobwebs—and he marks the rise of the water. Arthur places the edge of the ruler on the ground, stands on a milk crate he found in the alley behind the corner store, and marks one foot with his thumb, then two feet, three, and all the way to six and a half. There he draws a bold white line and writes "YEAR 2100." Beneath the line he writes "UNDERWATER."

After marking the buildings, Arthur likes to walk along the river. Not the big river that passes the famous buildings he once visited on a school trip, but a smaller river, one whose name few remember. Arthur doesn't know if it will be that water or different water, and he doesn't know how fast. Maybe the people will have time to move to other places, those the blue doesn't cover on the map. Or maybe it will come with a heavy rain, and his house will be like one of the houses on the TV after brown water covers the lawns and pours in through windows and leaves every rooftop a square island populated by people waving signs.

At home, Arthur trades his sister the main floor bedroom and a year of doing the dishes on her nights in exchange for her room in the attic. The room is long and slender and the ceilings vaulted. He places his books in neat rows along the walls and fixes his glow-in-the-dark solar system to his new ceiling. That night, over dinner, when their mother comes home from the restaurant with leftover noodles and tomato sauce, his sister calls him stupid.

"The upstairs is too hot anyway," she says.

His mother shakes her head. "As long as you're both happy, I don't care."

Arthur finishes his spaghetti and asks to be excused. He goes out into the night with his chalk and ruler. Arthur pulls the picnic table against the house, climbs atop, and measures six and a half feet. His mother will be gone, and his sister too, in her new room. But his small window is higher up, safe at that height. He can't see it from here because of all the houses and apartments, but Arthur knows how to walk to the river and he knows how the river will walk to him. He wants to know: How long will the rooftops float? And once the river swallows the houses and the street signs, will they change that river's name?

BALTIMORE

Kurt Rheinheimer's stories have appeared in more than 70 magazines, ranging from Redbook *to* Glimmer Train. *His first collection* Little Criminals *(EWU Press) won the Spokane Prize for Fiction and elicited this from* The New York Times Sunday Book Review: *"For Rheinheimer, geography is destiny." The story "Baltimore," part of that collection (and first published in* Michigan Quarterly Review, *Summer 1988), is also part of that syndrome, having been inspired by his first drive over the 1980s extension of the Southeast Freeway (MD 702) near Middle River, where he grew up. A 1969 grad, he lives with his wife Gail in Roanoke, Virginia, where he has been editor in chief at LeisureMedia360 since 1984. His second collection,* Finding Grace *(Press 53) was published in 2012; he is at work on a third.*

About a generation after the Beltway was finished and the land around it no longer appeared scraped and awkward next to the new highway, a new stretch was cut down through the marshy points and necks east of the city. The new highway rode tall and concrete-white above the salvage yards and filling stations and sheet metal shops that had evolved over the previous forty or fifty years to help serve the workers from the steel mills and the aircraft plants and the harbor itself. The new highway was an extension of the Beltway—a new outer loop—and connected the eastern part of the county with Interstate 95, the aorta of the East Coast interstates. So the new piece of highway tied the flat, forgotten east-county bogs and peninsulas with the whole country—to the big Midwestern manufacturing cities that had built the implements which now formed the big piles of rusting metal you saw every mile or so when you looked down from the new highway. It was as if the factories in Detroit and Gary and Akron had sent their finished goods eastward toward the sea, and along the way the machines had picked up more and more rust and disrepair until they had stalled completely in the junk yards all over the damp, short-treed lands along the upper reaches of the bay.

And on all of those peninsulas, the housing had grown up as patterned as the businesses. Whether you drove the twisting old blacktopped two-lanes built in the thirties or one of the new boulevard-size white roads that were slowly replacing them, you'd see the same evolution of houses. First built were the flat-roofed shanties put up between the wars and right down next to the water. Next, back a ways from the water, were rows and rows of small, cookie-cutter houses built during and just after World War II to accommodate the men who came up from the South to work in the factories and to start families. And last, spread along the boulevards, were fast-rise apartment buildings built in the sixties and seventies. They took on the dingy look of most of east county almost before they were completed, even before their lots started to fill with old GM and Ford cars.

Walker doesn't drive the new white interstate stretch. Hardly ever, anyway. He tells people he doesn't like looking down on the land where he grew up, and doesn't often go anywhere the new high bridge down over the harbor can take him anyway. He sticks to the roads he knew as a boy, as they snake their way through the lowlands to lead to all the diners and stores and low-slung bars where he takes his big gray Eastern Systems truck every day, where he earns his money on every Eastern Systems dumpster that goes up over the cab and empties into the big bin that rides behind him.

He's on the road early these days. He used to have trouble getting in on time, but now that Candy does aerobics every morning before she goes to work, he is up early and wanting to get going. She gets up before it's light, and spends close to an hour doing things to her hair before she goes to exercise. When she first started—almost four months ago—Walker got angry because he thought it must be something else that got her up so early in the morning. Who in her right mind would want to get up over an hour early to go jump around and sweat for forty-five minutes? She told him three other girls at the bank had been doing it for almost a year and had lost weight and even added an inch or so to their chest measurements, and didn't he want her to look good for him? She invited him to go too, and after about a month, he tried it once. He got up at ten till six and put on some cut-offs and tennis shoes, and took along his work clothes in a plastic grocery bag. She took him into the club—all smiles like it was her favorite place to be in the world, and introduced him to people left and right. What it was was almost non-stop jumping. Some of the music was okay—the Beatles and other old rock, and even a country song here and there (when they played the first one Candy grinned at him as wide as she could through her jumping and sweating, as if to say, see, this *is* great, because they play your favorite music)—but Walker got tired quickly. He felt awkward and gawky trying to follow the commands and movements through the loud music. He was tall—almost six-two—and kind of broad-shouldered. Most of the other men seemed to be small and flexible, like little gymnasts. Walker's stomach muscles wouldn't hold up for the abdominal exercises, and his arms got quivery real fast when he tried the bowling pins some of them used while they jumped around and ran in place.

But worse than all of that was the way the women looked. There were thirty-five or forty in the class, he guessed, and maybe half that many men. Most of the men were dressed in gym shorts and t-shirts—just like you'd see on guys playing pick-up basketball. But the women wore little one-piece things that looked like bathing suits with a pair of colored pantyhose underneath, or just a leotard, or little shorts-and-tops sets. And when they bent in all the different ways they bent, you would watch the men watching them. In just that one morning, Walker saw four women's panties under their little shorts. Later he told Candy that with all that twisting and pushing they did, he wasn't so sure the whole class wasn't just for singles to get warmed up for what they were going to do after work. Candy laughed and said there was no concept of sex—no concept of gender, she said, as if correcting herself—in the class, and Walker looked at her wondering where she was getting a word like that to use. No, she told him, nobody had ever made a pass at her the whole time she had been there. Didn't she have on her wedding band? And didn't she always go with at least two other girls—also married—from the bank? Geez, Frankie, she said, get out of the dark ages. She made him feel embarrassed in a boyish way.

He never went back, but since that day he has gotten up early with Candy while she gets her stuff ready—packing up just the right make-up colors she wants to go with the clothes she's picked out. She has a new purple gym bag with a thousand compartments in it. The purple color and the compartments make Walker uneasy, as if she is hiding little pieces of her life in there. Some mornings she says she feels like he's watching her, like she's a kid or something. And Walker thinks, yeah, maybe I am watching you. But he's not sure why. He knows he loves Candy more than he ever has. They've been married just over four years, and dated for more than two years before that, but there is something different now, something he feels he needs to watch, without quite knowing what it is.

He likes his Friday run. In fact, though he's been telling people for two years that he needs to do something more challenging, he likes the job. His mother tells him that driving a truck around all day is not making the best of his abilities, and Walker tells her she might be right, but in a way he's using his love of geography—that he likes driving all over the roads that show on the Geographical Survey Quadrangle maps he's been collecting since eighth grade. He agrees with his mother and Candy that he ought to go back to school—he went to college for a year and a half before he started driving one summer and never went back, and now he puts if off from fall to fall. The Friday run takes him a little north up into the part of the county where things haven't gotten so congested. It keeps him away from the Beltway for the most part, and from most of the big malls, where the bins are always getting blocked by parked cars. It is also the day that takes him by his old elementary school, and goes closest to Candy's bank.

There is something wrong with the hydraulics on the left side of Walker's lift, and so he goes into the day—into every day—dreading a real heavy load. There was one on Wednesday, at Carroll's Plumbing Supply, that the lift wouldn't handle. That's not just the pick-up money he loses, but there's the potential of a call to dispatch and then a reprimand to him for leaving a full bin full. They'll get on you for hitting bins too soon and for low daily totals, but the thing they hate worst is not emptying a full bin. Even if you have reported the hydraulics defect over and over again and nobody has fixed it. The bin at Walker's old school is light, though, and rides up over the cab and sets in smoothly and dumps clean, Walker can feel. It's a feeling he likes, knowing what the bin is doing. He used to tell Candy about how he could tell what was in them—how you could tell after you'd turned over ten thousand dumpsters what kind of stuff was in there, and how much it weighed. For a while she liked hearing that, and he liked lying in bed with her explaining how he had maneuvered the truck that day and how he'd been the top driver for the week—six hundred and eighteen bins in a week was his record, and only the drivers who worked downtown, where there was a dump every ten feet, had beaten it. And they'd talk in the dark about when he was going to get off the road and into a supervisory job. But once Candy got on with the bank—before that she had been daytime co-manager of the 7-Eleven just down from the apartment—and got to work on a computer, she was less interested. Walker wondered, somewhere deep inside him, if she had a feeling that his job wasn't as good as hers, even though he made twice as much money.

From the school he runs a string of three bars, a convenience store, a gas station, another convenience store, a restaurant, and then heads toward the Eastern Diner, where he stops for Friday coffee. The Eastern sits right on Route 40—up north and east of the city. The highway is Walker's favorite in the world because it is frozen in time, and the Eastern is a favorite for much the same reason, along with its feel of friendliness. There is a clipping from a magazine on the wall behind the cash register in the Eastern—showing a big, full-color picture of the outside of the restaurant, along with photographs of other highway diners that look like oversized house trailers with a lot of extra chrome on them. Candy told Walker that the magazine was mostly making fun of the way the diners look and that the people who ran the Eastern didn't even realize it. Walker told her maybe, but that the article also talked about them as forms of post-war highway art, so he wasn't sure.

Inside now, he hooks his cap over one of the posts on the coat tree just inside the door, and takes a seat at the counter. He knows most of the faces around him. Route drivers tend to end up at the same place at the same time every week, and so after a while you know who gets into what truck and what kind of doughnut he likes and whether he's divorced and what he thinks of the mayor. Walker takes a counter stool next to Dave Meyers, who has the Charles' Chips route for this end of the county. The last time Walker talked to Dave Meyers, he was talking about leaving the chip route and going on with Coke, but he worried about the weight he'd have to handle, and the possible strain on his back. "Not to mention my front," he said, loud enough for the waitresses to hear, and they'd all laughed.

"Still doing the light stuff, huh?" Walker says as he sits down.

"Yeah, what the hell," Meyers says with a smile. He doesn't say anything else about it and Walker says something about the Orioles getting rained out two days in a row. Meyers is the only person Walker knows who cares as much about baseball as he does.

"At least they're not losing," Meyers says. He tears two sugars open at the same time and dumps them into a new cup of coffee. "Face it, Frank, it's just not the same with them anymore." He taps his spoon against the side of his cup. "It started when Weaver left, got worse when he came back, and things haven't been right since."

"It might go back farther than that," Walker says. "Like back to when National Beer sold them. They were meant to be with National—a nice little regional beer running a nice little team the same way they ran the brewery—and so they built champions."

Meyers looks at Walker and smiles. "You've got a pretty bad case of them, don't you, Frank?" he says, and Walker smiles back. Meyers asks about the hydraulics on the truck.

"About the same," Walker says. "They won't replace anything until it's totally shot."

"I know the feeling," Meyers says.

They don't say anything while Walker orders coffee and whole wheat toast. He used to eat three or four doughnuts in here, but Candy has convinced him that he's getting to the age where he needs to be thinking about his metabolism. "Metabolism?" he said to her when she told him that, and she said damn right—metabolism. One day it's *gender*, the next day it's *metabolism*. She told him one day soon his body wasn't going to burn stuff up as fast as it used to and wham, he was going to weigh two hundred pounds before he knew it. Not to mention the strain he was putting on his heart with all that lousy food he ate all the time.

"How's Jane Fonda?" Meyers says, as if he's reading Walker's thoughts.

"About the same too," Walker says. "Every morning at the club, half the morning with exercise tapes at home on Saturday and Sunday. Your basic fanatic."

Meyers tears off two more sugars and dumps them into new coffee. He shakes his head. "Better than my weekend, anyway," he says.

Walker doesn't say anything.

"At least you had somebody around to watch," Meyers says.

Walker still doesn't say anything. If a guy is getting ready to talk about his wife or his girl, you let him pick the pace. You don't go asking a lot of questions until he shows you it's okay.

"I mean it's pretty damn empty at my place right now," Meyers says.

"No kidding," Walker says. He can't remember Meyers' girl's name right now, but knows Meyers has been with her ever since Walker met him.

"Nope, no kidding," Meyers says. "Last weekend. Saturday night. I'm thinking we should go rent a movie or something and I hear her back in the bedroom scraping around—I thought she was rearranging the furniture—and pretty soon she's standing there in the hallway with two suitcases and is telling me she'll be back for the rest of her stuff." He pauses, takes a sip of coffee. Walker shakes his head, hoping Meyers will notice.

"And I'm standing there with no idea what in hell is going on," Meyers says. "'It's better to do it clean, Dave,' she says to me." He blows air through his teeth. "She's dressed to kill—like she's on her way out the door and straight to Acapulco or someplace—and she's telling me it's better to do it clean. And you know what? I never even asked. I didn't want to know his name. I didn't want to think about her taking off for some new place with some jerk so he could rub his hands all over her pussy hair—I just didn't want to know." He takes another sip of coffee, looking around as if to make sure the waitresses didn't hear the last part.

"Damn," Walker says softly. He tries to picture the clothes, and when he does—a fancy, light purple dress that is low-cut and has a slit part-way up one leg—he envisions Candy in it, standing out in front of the apartment next to her Paseo telling Walker it's cleaner this way. He picks up his coffee to help get rid of the picture.

"Damn is right," Meyers says. "Two and a half years. Two point five years of my life I gave to her because I thought she asked for it. You know where I met her? At a track meet. Can you believe that? I took my son from my first marriage to this meet for like all ages at the Armory track and here is this gorgeous woman in these matching yellow sweats—I mean the sweetest pair of sweats you ever saw. Lemon-colored, like. She won the 440 in those things for her age group—like she knew better than to take them off even for the race." Meyers stops talking and looks at his coffee. "What the hell," he says, and slaps Walker lightly on the shoulder. "You don't need this crap, Frankie," he says, "and neither do I." He looks up from the counter at the waitresses and asks one of them why his doughnuts always have the biggest holes. They all laugh with him even though it's as standard a line as there is along the counter in the Eastern. Meyers talks a little about the new mall up in Northwest County and then says it's time he got back on the route.

"It takes more hustle than it used to, doesn't it, Frank?" he says to Walker as he slides off the stool, and Walker agrees and tells Meyers he'll see him next Friday.

Back in the truck, Walker listens to the morning disc jockey joke with the news girl about her date last night, right before she starts reading the international news. The more Walker thinks back over what Dave Meyers said, the more he considers the possibility of dropping by to take his wife to lunch—anywhere she wants. The last time he did that— maybe five or six Fridays back—she got a little edgy about that big dirty truck parked right there in the bank lot, and once Walker got almost all the way over being angry about that, he told her okay, he'd park the truck somewhere dirty and walk to her pristine bank to take her to lunch. Then she congratulated him on using the word *pristine*, even though he didn't mean it, and Walker turned around and walked out and went to lunch by himself. When they made up she told him she really did feel bad about the truck thing, and knew how much he liked it, and that was just fine with her. She said she had no right to judge what he liked, just that management really did like to keep the front of the lot kind of clean-looking. Walker said he understood. And as he was going to sleep that night—after they'd made love better than they had for a long time—he had this sort of half-dream/half-vision of himself rolling up to one of those little branch banks—it wasn't Candy's exact bank—

and scooping it up with the forks and dumping all the money and the cranky tellers and the little rack of information flyers into the bin, and then setting the bank back down on the lot with a bunch of cracks in the walls and the sign all mashed. He never told her about that.

In fact, there's a lot he doesn't tell her anymore. He has been thinking of maybe going out west later in the summer— when the Orioles travel out there—maybe taking in a game or two in Seattle and then driving up into Canada for a few days. Actually, for all his love of geography, he hates to travel, and has turned Candy down on every trip she's ever proposed for them except the one to her uncle's cabin in Maine right after they got married. Since then they've been to Ocean City each summer, but nowhere else. Maybe the reason Walker doesn't tell Candy about his travel plans is that he knows he really doesn't want to do it—knows that if he went, he'd be going as much to spite her as for his own pleasure. She knows he likes geography and he has been looking for ways to prove it to her and learn more for himself. He watches the flyers from the community colleges and continuing education programs, but they never have anything. You can take Polynesian cooking or Lotus computers or advanced fashion theory, for God's sake, but not geography. Candy takes a class almost every fall and spring now, usually in banking stuff or computers, although last spring she took one in photography that she ended up not finishing. For a while Walker thought it might be a warm-up to having a baby, because she talked about taking pictures of kids, but when they talked about it she said she needed to get off the counter full-time first—maybe make assistant manager or something—because then they have more invested in you

and you have a better chance of coming back where you want
to.

Walker takes care of his next four stops with no
problems—no cars blocking things and no big weights. On the
radio they are well into the dead part of the day—the soft
oldies for housewives—and Walker slides in a Bob Seger
tape. Bob Seger sings about being older now but still running
against the wind, and Walker thinks about how people—from
his younger brother to his in-laws—have been giving him
grief over Bob Seger for years, telling him to broaden his
horizons a little. But to Walker's mind, nothing better has
come along. He tells people that the secret to a good song is a
nice piano line, a persistent backbeat and a plaintive voice
spread just right over the melody line. And who can do that
better than Bob Seger, he asks people.

He is aware, as he dumps the Turkey Neck Inn, that he
really is going to the bank. It's a little early, but that will give
her time to change any plans she might have made. He'll park
the truck three or four blocks away, walk in and surprise her,
and tell her to aim the Paseo toward the healthiest lunch she
can think of, because he's ready. In his head he rearranges his
route to take in a machine shop and two restaurants on the
way to the bank, and then decides once the Seger tape is
finished, he'll play one of the tapes Candy has been trying for
months to get him to listen to. It's New Age music, she says,
and it's really relaxing. She plays the tapes in the kitchen
sometimes when she's paying her part of the bills. The music's
okay with him—some nice tunes and guitar and piano lines—
but there are two things he doesn't like all that much about it.
One is he wonders if it might not just be elevator music
moved up a notch or two—you know, where the music doesn't

say anything but doesn't get in the way much either. And two, it is pretty much like everything else Candy likes these days—kind of too classy and stylish for her own good or her own taste. Like she's really not quite picking it out for herself. He never did get around to doing it, but one day when he was out on his route and was thinking about her at the bank smiling like crazy at everybody because she wanted a better job, he decided to make a list of all the things she used to like and the things she likes now. The first thing he thought of was beer. She used to like beer the same as he did—good beers like Heineken and Molson—but now she'll hardly touch one. She went to wine coolers first, and lately has pretty much changed over completely to white wine. Same with TV. Not even the good ten o'clock dramas anymore. Now it's books and magazines for her. Not that he has anything against them—just that he's never quite sure what he can suggest for the two of them to do together anymore.

At his last dump before the bank—a little sub shop called George's that sits kind of by itself along a road that has had the traffic drained away by the new interstate—Walker makes the dump and then slides down off the seat to use George's restroom, comb his hair and get a Coke before he hits the bank. George is not quite as friendly as he used to be when all twelve stools and all six booths were jammed every day from 11:15 until two o'clock, but he knows he still makes the best cheesesteak on this side of town. Walker eats there at least once a week, and when he goes in now he tells George how he's taking his wife to lunch—this as a way of apologizing for not sitting down with a cheesesteak. George gestures with a wave of his hand, and gives Walker the Coke on the house.

Near the bank, Walker parks the truck at the edge of Hale's Point Shopping Center. It is an old, decrepit strip center—the first one built in this part of the county, and in the time since it was put up—soon after the war—maybe six other malls have gone up in the area, making Hale's Point more and more obsolete-looking as its sidewalks crack and its buildings never get repainted. On the Hale's Point lot the truck does not look so big and dirty, he tells himself. It kind of fits in with the old laundromat and the IGA grocery store that are the closest things the center has to anchor stores. Candy's bank is two blocks away, set right on the corner next to a brand-new, long-armed traffic signal. Walker used to put air in his bicycle tires in the old Gulf station that sat, all through his boyhood, on the lot where the bank is now.

He goes in smiling, though he does not know any of the people at this branch very well. He doesn't see Candy at the counter, and scans the two desks over to the right, where you open new accounts. He pauses, and then decides to go ahead and ask. At the only teller slot without a customer, Bernice Walsh tells him Candy just left for lunch. She looks at her watch. "Couldn't've been more than three minutes ago," she says. "I think they were going downtown to eat. There's that training seminar this afternoon, and so I think they were going on down and staying." She smiles too nicely at Walker, who is embarrassed. But because he does not want to give up on his plan, he asks her if she knows where they planned to eat.

"Well," she says blandly. She is too old to be a bank teller, it occurs to Walker. Ladies with bluish hair are supposed to work the desks, or maybe the downtown counters. "Frances," Mrs. Walsh calls across the floor to one of the little desks, "you know where Candace and them went to lunch?"

Walker feels more warmth in his face, not just at her yelling out, but also because she said *Candace*. It's such a hotsy-totsy name—like Candice Bergen—and makes Walker uneasy. Candy got these little return address stickers in the mail and they say "Frank and Candace Walker" on the first line, instead of "Mr. and Mrs. Frank Walker," like on the old ones. Frances calls back that she knows it was down at the harbor someplace, but she's not sure exactly where.

Back in the truck, Walker decides he is far enough ahead for the day to push on and try downtown, as much as he hates the traffic lights as you drive down there. They are bad enough out in the county, but the closer you get to town, the thicker and more poorly timed they are. Plus the whole feel of the inner harbor makes him uncomfortable. As he takes the truck off the Hale's Point lot he decides to work on not being angry, on thinking about still maybe being able to surprise her for lunch. She used to surprise him in lots of ways like that. Some mornings he'd get in the truck and find candy or baseball cards or something silly on the seat. He never knew how she got them there, but they made him feel good. Which is the way he started thinking about this lunch. He has given her a hard time about her self-improvement stuff, when it really is all good, and he wants her to know that. Now though, on his way into the city, he is beginning to worry—beginning to feel self-conscious about walking into a restaurant while she is sitting there with a bunch of people from the bank. The New Age tape is still in the player, and Walker recognizes a version of "Greensleeves." It sounds good to him, but it takes him back to the list of things about Candy that he never quite wrote down. He left off with books. Lately she's been reading this one where the main guy is separated from his wife, and takes his dirty clothes into the shower with him so he can stomp them clean while he takes a shower, and get two things done at one time. Candy tells him the author is from right there in Baltimore, and that at least the guy had a system for things. There are times when Walker wonders if she is trying to tell him something—maybe wants him to get ready to be left behind or something. That one day she'll come home with really strange stuff—maybe a Beethoven album and some soft smelly cheese wrapped in a little triangle and a big loaf of dark rye bread, and Walker just won't know her anymore—she'll be a whole new person. Sometimes he feels that way about the city itself. People talk about the new restaurants and the shops down by the harbor, and the new stadium and new pride and sense of itself that the city has, and Walker can't understand it all the way. He's been downtown with Candy to eat, and even to see a play. He's been down there with her on festival days to get the "feel" of it she talks about so much. But to him it is all sort of flimsy and unreal. The things he remembers best from downtown have to do with sports. He and his friends used to go to the Civic Center back before the basketball team moved to Washington. They'd go see Earl Monroe and Wes Unseld, and people would cheer like crazy, and then spill out into the street on a cold winter night and still be screaming. It felt exciting and dangerous to be there. Now it feels sort of sterilized to Walker. Or the Colts. He is too young to remember the late fifties and early sixties, but there were great teams even into the seventies, with Johnny Unitas leading the way. Now you read about Johnny Unitas in *Baltimore Magazine* and he is talking about investments and good neighborhoods and getting shafted by the Colts, and

Walker doesn't read any more. Even the Orioles seem sort of corporate these days.

The city, he decides as he gets close to downtown, just doesn't feel as strong to him, as masculine, as it used to. It gets written up in magazines for the new retail and culture coming in, and people still talk about the amazing rebirth, but he doesn't quite trust it. Much as he fears the heavy dumps because of the hydraulic problem, he thinks the overall tonnage of stuff he's dumped over the years has gone steadily down, as if all the big manufacturing plants—the steel and industrial parts—have been replaced by little cute stuff that people put on their mantels for a few weeks and then trash, or send to each other in the mail and then trash. He hates it that so many maps show Washington and Philadelphia, but not Baltimore. And that so many people now talk about the Washington-Baltimore area. In that order. He lives in fear that one day they'll take the Orioles away too, leaving a once-major Eastern Seaboard city with nothing but a transplanted football team and a little toy indoor soccer team for pro-sports.

Near the harbor area, the traffic is not as bad as he thought it would be. They've gotten things all one-wayed to the extent that traffic flows pretty well. Walker makes a swoop down near the water and then drives up into the streets a few blocks away, where all the glitter and shininess hasn't been put in, and it still looks pretty much like harbor-area slums—the way it all used to. He finds a place to leave the truck—in a head-in parking area where he takes up a space and a half—and starts walking down toward the harbor. All around him the black kids on skateboards are fast and athletic, jumping curbs and rising suddenly into the air as if they had a ramp or had suddenly turned off the force of gravity for a few seconds. It occurs to Walker that they have changed too—maybe in reaction to the harbor—as if they have built their skills in order to better show off for the tourists.

Walker decides to try the White Gull Restaurant first. It's the one Candy talks about most. You go in and build your own lunch—all kinds of fresh vegetables and sprouts and cheeses and meats and every kind of bread you can think of. Six or eight kinds of mustard alone. Walker makes his way through the crowd, not remembering exactly where the restaurant is. He thinks it is down near where *The Pride of Baltimore* used to dock before it blew away in a storm. Candy got all bothered when that happened, and when Walker teased her that it was just a cheap re-creation of the real ship, and didn't have any business out on the high seas, they had a big fight that lasted most of two days. Walker cannot find the White Gull, and begins to look in every restaurant he comes to. He does not look carefully, but steps inside and glances around until someone starts up to ask if it will be just one for lunch, and then turns to leave. He is hoping that Candy will see him before he sees her—that she'll call out to him to come over and sit down. He goes into six or seven restaurants that way, trying to let his height work to his advantage. With each one he becomes more discouraged. Two million people in the metropolitan area and he thinks he is going to drive down here at lunch on a Friday and find one of them? When he's not even totally sure she's here, and even if she is, that she really wants to see him anyway? As Walker cranes his neck in The Cutting Board, he wonders if she thinks of him kind of like she does the truck—a little too big and scruffy to go with the bank, or maybe even to fit in her life. He shaved his beard a year or so ago for that very reason, but still likes his hair a little long at the neck, and with his bushy eyebrows and dark complexion, he feels he looks a little unkempt anyway.

Each time he comes out of a restaurant he tells himself he will look in one more and then quit. He does this five times before he really does turn away from the harbor and start back toward the truck. He is hungry and angry, and needs something to do with the energy that creates. As he gets past the tourists in their bright clothes and back into skateboard territory, he wishes he knew how to use a skateboard—that he could zoom downtown into the business district, take an elevator up to the main conference room at Candy's bank, and then do a few spinning, airborne moves in the middle of the conference table while they tried to talk about customer service. He starts to jog toward the truck once he is all the way out of the crowd. By the time he reaches it, there is sweat dripping down into his eyes. Inside the truck he takes out the wimpy tape and reaches back into the glove compartment for some good basic rock and roll. George Thoroughgood and the Delaware Destroyers. He revs the engine a few times to make sure he's cleared the skateboarders from behind him, and backs the truck out to aim it straight down toward the harbor. As he starts down the street, his eye catches the worn-silver ends of the truck's big forks as they stick up into the air— forks that have lifted ten thousand big metal bins of every kind of Baltimore garbage you can think of, not to mention the body of a woman in a murder case two years back that Walker helped solve when he thought one night about what a great place a dumpster would be to hide a body. All that lifting and dumping has worn and sharpened the ends of the forks, as if someone had sat up nights honing and polishing weapons until they were just the right tone and temper for battle. Walker likes having them there as the truck heads for the harbor. At the first traffic light he hits red, he brings them down a little from their straight-up position to run out from the sides of the truck, as if they are pointed swords to clear the way for him. That way, if he does decide to take out a restaurant on the edge of the water, then the forks will catch the sunlight just before they crash through the cute-curtained windows and send all those little chunks of cheese and meat and olive and carrot down to float their way on out into the cold gray water of the harbor.

MAYHEM

Jamie Shaw is the author of the Mayhem *series, a New Adult romance series that follows the members of an up-and-coming rock band. Born and raised in South Central Pennsylvania, she holds a B.A. in Professional Writing from York College of Pennsylvania and an M.S. in Professional Writing from Towson University. She's an incurable night owl, a loyal drinker of white chocolate mochas, and a passionate enthusiast of all things romance. When she's not being goofy with her young son or crafting novels with swoon-worthy leading men, she loves interacting with her readers. Her goal with every book is to add a new name to their book boyfriend lists. The following passage is from the first chapter of the first book in the* Mayhem *series.*

"I can't believe I let you talk me into this." I tug at the back of the stretchy nylon skirt my best friend squeezed me into, but unless I want to show the tops of my panties instead of the skin of my thighs, there is nothing I can do. After casting yet another uneasy glance at the long line of people stretched behind me on the sidewalk, I shift my eyes back to the sun-warmed fabric pinched between my fingers and grumble, "The least you could've done was let me wear some leggings."

Dee just laughs and bats my hands away from the material. "Stop your bitching, Ro. You'll thanks me when we're old and gray and you look back on this night and realize that once, just *once*," she shoves her pointer finger in my face to emphasize the lonely number, "you actually flaunted that hot little body of yours before it got all old and saggy."

"I look ridiculous," I complain, pushing her finger away and rolling my eyes for good measure. I look like Dee's closet drank too much and threw up on me. She somehow talked me into wearing this mini-skirt—which skintight doesn't even begin to describe—and a hot-pink top that shows more cleavage than should be legal. The front of it drapes all the way down to just above my navel, and the bottom exposes a pale sliver of skin between the hem of the shirt and the top of my skirt. The hot-pink fabric matches my killer hot-pink heels.

Literally, killer. Because I know I am going to fall on my face and die.

I'm fiddling with the skirt again when one of the guys near us in line leans in close, a jackass smile on his lips, "I think you look hot."

Of course he thinks I look hot—I look like a freaking prostitute!

"I have a boyfriend," I counter, but Dee just scoffs at me.

"She means *thank you*," she shoots back, chastising me with her tone until the guy flashes us another arrogant smile— he's stuffed into an appallingly snug graphic-print tee that might as well say "douchebag" in its shiny metallic lettering, and even Dee cannot help but make a face before we both turn away.

She and I are the first ones in line for the show tonight, standing by the doors to Mayhem under the red-orange glow of a setting summer sun. She has been looking forward to this night for weeks, but I was more excited about it before my boyfriend of three years had to back out.

"Brady is a jerk," she says, and all I can do is sigh because I wish those two could just get along. Deandra and I have been best friends since preschool, but Brady and I have been dating since my sophomore year of high school and living together for the past two months. "He should be here to appreciate how gorgeous you look tonight, but nooo, it's always work first with him."

"He moved all the way here to be with me, Dee. Cut him some slack, alright?"

She grumbles her frustration until she catches me touching my eyelids for the zillionth time tonight. Yanking my fingers away, she orders, "stop messing with it. You'll smear."

I stare down at my shadowy fingertips and rub them together. "Tell me the truth," I say, flicking the clumped powder away. "Do I look like a clown?"

"You look smoking hot!" she assures me with a smile. "If I was a lesbian, you'd be in trouble!"

I laugh until Douchebag leans in again, popping our personal bubble with his enormously hooked nose. "Don't let that stop you."

We both glare at him so sharply that he immediately stumbles a step back, his obnoxiously red sneakers suddenly becoming the most fascinating things he has ever seen. Dee and I turn back around, glancing at each other and trying not to laugh. She playfully elbows me in the arm, and I chuckle and nudge her right back. My smile settles back into place and

I finally feel like I am beginning to loosen up when a guy walks right past us like he is going to cut in line. In dark shades and a baggy black knit cap that droops in the back, he flicks a cigarette to the ground, and my eyes narrow on him.

Dee and I have been waiting for way too long to let some self-entitled jerk cut in front of us, so when he knocks on the door to the club, I force myself to speak up.

"They're not letting people in yet," I say, hoping he takes the hint. Even with my skyscraper heels, I feel dwarfed standing next to him. He has to be at least six-foot-two, maybe taller.

He turns his head toward me and lowers his shades, smirking like something's funny. His wrist is covered with string bracelets and rubber bracelets and a thick leather cuff, and three of his fingernails on each hand are painted black. But his eyes are what steal the words from my lips—a greenish shade of light gray. They are stunning.

When the door opens, he turns to it and locks hands with the bouncer.

"You're late," the bouncer says, and the guy in the shades laughs and slips inside. Once he disappears, Dee pushes my shoulders.

"Oh my GOD! Do you know who you were just talking to?!"

I shake my head.

"That was *Adam* EVEREST! He's the lead freaking singer of the band we're here to see!"

Oh. . .God. . .No. "You're kidding. . ."

She shakes her head, stifling a laugh. "Did you see the way he looked at you?!"

"Like I'm an idiot!"

She pulls me in for a hug and finally lets loose the laughter she has been holding in.

"You couldn't have told me?"

Dee squeezes me tight. "He was standing right there! What was I supposed to do?!"

She laughs even harder. "Oh, babe, I'm sorry! That was—" Her body is still shaking with laughter when I feel her lift a hand behind my back to wipe a tear from her eye.

I groan and finish her sentence, "The most mortifying moment of my life."

"Come on, you've had worse. *Much* worse." She pulls away and grins at me. "Do you remember that time at David Miller's house when—"

"Okay, Dee? Not making me feel better here!"

She chuckles to herself as she applies another coat of shiny pink lip gloss and then shoots her hand forward to do the same to me. "We'll call that the first of the many epic memories we're going to make tonight."

"Why in God's name would I want to remember that?" I ask after puckering my lips.

"Because you talked to Adam Everest!"

A tiny voice chimes from behind me. "Your friend is right," the girl says, nodding to herself. "And he looked right at you. He *smiled* at you."

"Isn't he gorgeous?!" Dee asks, never one to miss an opportunity to gush over boys. She and the girl behind us start gossiping about Adam while I lose myself in my thoughts. I just talked to a rock star, a freaking rock star. Granted, I had no idea who he was, but damn, he did look the part. If I could go back, what would I have said? Probably nothing, and then I never would have seen that smile, or those eyes.

"You're blushing," Dee says, breaking me from the memory.

"It's hot out here!" I lie.

"You're practically naked, and it is *not* that hot." Her lips pull into a knowing grin, which only makes my skin burn even pinker.

I am saved when the door to Mayhem opens and I practically trip over myself to get inside. I have a boyfriend, and even though I am sure I will never speak to Adam again, I really should not be replaying the moment in my mind wishing I would have done things differently.

In the dim haze of the club, a bouncer glances at our fake IDs and stamps our hands, and Dee pulls me straight to the bar. She holds up two fingers to signal the bartender and orders us two dirty girl scouts, but she has not even lowered her hand yet when a random guy sidles up next to her, threatening to choke us with his cologne.

"You look a little too. . ." his eyes scan over us, making me feel like I am wearing even less than I already am, "*mature* to be Girl Scouts, but I will believe anything a girl as pretty as you tells me." Corniest pick-up line ever. He grins like a cheeseball. "What can I get you ladies to drink?"

Dee turns to me and mouths "Just go with it," so I do. And, voilà, free shots.

Cheeseball, who is apparently named Vinnie, pays for the first round, and some guy named. . .well, I have no idea what the hell his name is, buys the second round, and then Dee is dragging me onto the crowded dance floor. In advance of the show, the club is booming with house music, and it's fueling her hyper mood.

I laugh as she bounces in front of me with her wrists on my shoulders. She looks incredible, as always, in a ruffled blue mini-skirt and super low-cut white top. It is backless, flaunting the golden tan she has worked for all summer. Her long chocolate-brown curls are bouncing from side to side with the beat, and I finally give in and drop it low, rising back up ass-first like a freaking stripper. Dee laughs at me and twirls around with her hands in the air, and then we are lost to the alcohol pumping through our blood and the music vibrating beneath our feet.

By the third song, my thick blonde waves are glued to the back of my neck. I flip them away as Dee bends low and rolls her ass against my thighs. We are both laughing so hard that I am surprised we have not fallen over yet. My sides cramp like I am out of practice.

When I feel stiff jeans press up behind me, my smile vanishes. I try to inch away, pressing tighter against Dee, but the jeans follow, and then grabby hands grip my sides. The floor is so crowded that I would not even be able to turn around without being pressed flush against whatever creeper is behind me, so I press my mouth into Dee's hair and tell her I am heading to the bar. When I begin pushing through the crowd, her fingers curl around mine and she follows. Together, we find our way off the floor.

"What gives?" she shouts once we break free from the overheated crowd.

"Some asshole was getting way too touchy-feel."

"Damn. Was he hot?"

"I didn't get a look at him."

"Well next time, if he's cute, send him my way." She winks, and I laugh and brace my hands on the bar, still trying to catch my breath. Dee leans back against it, propping her elbows on top with her chest out in the most casually provocative pose she can muster. It works like a charm, because within seconds, two guys are in front of her.

"You girls looked amazing out there."

I am still facing away from them, not interested. When they ask us to dance, Dee reaches over and grabs my hand.

I turn around and give the guys an apologetic smile. "I have a boyfriend."

"You go," I insist, nudging her toward the dance floor.

"You sure?"

"Yeah, go. I'm going to hang here for a while. I need a break."

Her perfectly shaped eyebrows pull together. "I'll stay if you want me to. . ."

I know she would, but I shoo her from the bar anyway. "GO!"

She laughs, her brown eyes sparkling with contagious excitement. "Okay, I'll be back soon!"

Both boys follow her like puppy dogs, and I smile to myself, knowing they are both in trouble.

After losing sight of her, I pull my phone out of my clutch purse and sigh when I realize there are no missed calls from Brady. It is almost ten o'clock, and I really wish he would have called to say goodnight. But he probably knew it would be loud in here, and he was probably exhausted from working all day. He is out of town for the weekend again, on yet another long-distance job for the advertising firm his uncle owns, and I have grown accustomed to sitting by the phone—

he joined the company right after graduating, when I was still a sophomore, and traveling to meet with clients has always been a big part of the job. Still, the trips have been more and more frequent lately, and they always feel way longer than they really are.

My fingers type a quick text.

Miss you. Having a blast but wish you were here! Hope your day wasn't too rough. Can't wait to see you tomorrow! I love you.

I tuck my phone back into my purse and turn around, laughing when I spot Dee in the crowd, sandwiched between her two club gorillas and outshining them both. She looks amazing, and she knows it. In high school, she was not on the cheerleading squad, but she dated most of the football team. Most of the other girls hated her, but she did not care and neither did I. She had a well-earned bad reputation, but she never tried to be anyone she was not. She is *real*, and I love that about her.

When a stool opens up at the bar, I immediately dive into it. My last drink is long gone, so I pull out my paper-thin wallet and flag the bartender.

I order another vodka cranberry and try to pull out cash to pay, but before I can manage, a thick hand covers mine. "A fox like you should never have to pay for her own drink." The guy uses his other hand to slip the bartender a credit card, and I sigh, looking up into plain brown eyes deeply set into a meathead face.

"I have a boyfriend," I say, trying not to sound rude but feeling pretty exasperated. With the number of times I am having to repeat that tonight, it would have been easier to get words tattooed on my forehead.

"Is he here?"

"No. . ."

"Then he's an idiot. Dance with me." The guy grabs my drink with one hand and tries to coax me off my stool with the other.

"No thanks."

"Aw, come on," he persists, refusing to stop tugging at my hand. "Don't make me beg."

"Sorry." I pull out his grip and settle back on my seat.

"Why the hell would you come here dressed like that if you're just going to be a tease?" he snaps, but I ignore him completely, flagging the bartender again.

When the meathead calls me a slut and walks away—with my drink—I roll my eyes and order another, which I pay for myself before any other assholes have the chance to intercede. If I am a slut, then Mother Teresa was too, because I might as well be her. Brady's father is a pastor, so Brady made the decision for both of us that we would be waiting until marriage—whenever that's going to be. He agreed to live together, under the condition that we have separate bedrooms, but second base is getting harder and harder to stick to. I know I am only eighteen, but we have been in a committed relationship for three years already, and now we are living together and, well, what the hell is he waiting for?

I gradually lose myself to people-watching while I sip on my drink and wait for Dee to tire herself out. The group beside me at the bar all look like college kids. They seem nice, and it makes me hopeful that I will make at least a few new friends on Monday. Next to them is a girl dressed even sluttier than I am, surrounded by three guys who are all shamelessly hitting on her. I wonder if the guys are friends with each other, and I am curious to see which will win the little competition they have got going on. The one with the blond faux-hawk is pretty damn cute; my money would be on him.

His eyes lift to catch me staring, and he smiles at me. I look away before he gets the wrong impression and decides to come over.

Next to him is a guy with his back to me, talking to a girl with bright purple eye shadow. She is gorgeous, with rich brown hair styled in a long bob. She laughs at something he says, and he places his hand on her forearm, caressing it tenderly with his thumb, giving her all the right signals. She is leaning slightly toward him, batting her lashes and brushing her fingers through her hair. I am still staring when the guy turns toward the bar to order another drink.

And my heart shatters into a million jagged pieces.

Brady.

I blink, for a second believing that I cannot trust my vision. I rub my eyes and stare harder, but it is definitely him. What the fuck is he doing here?

Maybe he came here to meet me. I scramble to check my phone.

No missed texts. No missed calls. I look from him to my phone and back again, remembering that Dee had mistakenly told me that we were going to a different club across town and that is what I told Brady. He did not expect me to be here. With my eye on my phone, I type another text.

Are you still working?

I watch as he pulls his phone from his shirt pocket, checks it, and then tucks it away. The girl he is with says something, and he leans in close to her ear, then kisses her cheek.

Maybe they are just friends. Please just be friends.

I watch as they laugh, as they talk, and then Brady leans in and kisses her. And it is not a friend kiss. He does not even come up for air, and I cannot remember the last time he kissed me like that. I am practically falling of my stool before I know it, scrambling to find an exit door before I turn into a blubbering mess right there in front of everyone. I can barely see through the cloud of tears in my eyes as my hands push past people who stare at me or throw curses my way. Finally, I slam into a big metal door and fly outside just as a sob bubbles outs of my throat.

I brace my hands on the cold star railing and struggle to breathe. I suck in air, desperately trying to regain some semblance of composure. How could he? How could he?!

Three years. Three fucking years. He asked me to move in with him! We live together, for God's sake. I have never done *anything* to deserve this. I would not even dance with those perfectly nice guys inside!

My knees feel like they are going to fail me, so I sit down on the top cement stair and curl my arms arounds my legs. It has gotten chilly, but that is the least of my problems. What am I going to do? I cannot sleep under the same roof as him tomorrow night. I cannot. I just cannot.

It is pitch-dark except for a single light hanging above the door and some overhead lights across the parking lot. Bugs swarm in the spotlight above me, and normally I would be paranoid about being so close to them since I am allergic to pretty much all insect bites known to man, but right now, I do not care. They can eat me alive; hopefully they finish the job.

I reach my hand up to wipe the tears from my cheeks, realizing for the first time that I have been crying. God, what I am going to do? Should I go back in there? Should I tell Dee? She will kill him.

I bury my face in my knees and let myself really cry then, sobs racking my body. I loved him. I loved him with every piece of me. I would have given him forever. My whole future. . .

When the door opens behind me, I sit up straight and hurriedly sniff in my tears as I wipe my shaking fingers across my slippery cheeks. I hear the flick of a lighter, and then someone sits down next to me on the stairs, puffing a cigarette. When I look over at him, I nearly choke.

He gazes back at me, starting at my hot-pink heels and then raking his way up, and then he chuckles. "Are they letting people in yet?"

Adam. He has ditched the shades and cap and now his dark brown hair is framing his gorgeous face, stretching almost to his chin. I look away quickly, hoping he cannot tell I have been crying.

"Sorry about that," I say. And I hear the hoarse sadness in my voice, but I could not keep it out.

When he reaches over and brushes my tangled hair away from my eyes, I tense.

"Is everything okay?" he asks, and I half laugh. No, everything is not okay.

"Everything's fine."

"Then why have you been crying?"

"No reason."

"You get all dolled up to sit outside of rock shows crying by yourself?"

I lift my gaze to stare into his eyes, and something in them makes me believe he really cares. Or maybe that is just what I want to see, but I suddenly need to tell someone. "My boyfriend's in there."

"And?"

"With another girl. I just caught him cheating."

Adam takes a deep puff of his cigarette, nodding as he sighs it back out. "Want me to fuck him up?"

I laugh, and he smiles at me. "Would you?"

"If you want me to."

"Why?"

He shrugs. "Because I offered."

"Why'd you offer?"

"Who knows why I do anything I do?" He stares at me while I wait for an answer. "I just do."

That is a good enough explanation for me, so I look back to my knees again, letting out a shaky breath. I cannot believe I just laughed. At a time like this, Adam Everest made me laugh.

"Anyway, your boyfriend is a dumbass," he says out of nowhere.

"How do you know?"

His gray-green eyes wash over me. "Look at you."

I blush like hell, but I know he is just trying to make me feel better. "You thought I was an idiot when you first saw me."

Adam chuckles and shakes his head. "I thought you were cute as a peach." His lips hold a cigarette in his mouth as he stands up, holding a hand down to me. My heart stops; Adam Everest is offering me his hand. In faded denim jeans, all torn up at the knees, and a fit olive-green button-down rolled up to his elbows, he makes my heart race to a nonexistent finish line. "Come on, Peach."

I take his hand, and he lifts me to my feet, leading me away from the building.

"Where are we going?"

"To get you a drink. I think you need one."

"I've had a few," I think out loud, slowing to a stop.

Adam gazes over his shoulder at me, his eyebrow cocked when he asks, "Are you saying you don't want another?"

I take a moment to consider his question.

Just a moment, and then I keep walking.

POETRY

THE CATS IN KRASINSKI SQUARE

Karen Hesse was born in Baltimore in 1952. She attended Towson University (then Towson State College) in 1969 as a theater major; however, she ultimately graduated from the University of Maryland at College Park as an English major. Ms. Hesse was a MacArthur Fellow in 2002 and also won the Newbery Medal in 1998. She currently lives with her husband in Vermont and has two daughters. Karen Hesse's books for children and young adults are marked by her use of free verse and her use of historic settings of time and place.

The cats
come
from the cracks in the Wall,
the dark corners,
the openings in the rubble.
They know
I can offer only
a gentle hand,
a tender voice.
They have no choice but to come.
They belonged once to someone.
They slept on sofa cushions

and ate from crystal dishes.
They purred,
furrowing the chests,
nuzzling the chins of their beloveds.
Now they have no one to kiss their
velvet heads. I whisper,
"I have no food to spare."
The cats don't care.
I can keep my fistful of bread,
my watery soup, my potato,
so much more
than my friend Michal gets
behind the Wall of the Ghetto.
The cats don't need me feeding them.
They get by nicely on mice.
I look like any child
playing with cats
in the daylight
in Warsaw,
my Jewish armband burned with the rags I wore
when I escaped the Ghetto.
I wear my Polish look,
I walk my Polish walk.
Polish words float from my lips
and I am almost safe,
almost invisible,
moving through Krasinski Square
past the dizzy girls riding the merry-go-round.
My brave sister,
Mira,
all that I have left of our family,

my brave sister
tells me the plan,
the newest plan
to smuggle food inside the Ghetto.
Her friends will come on the train,
carrying satchels
filled
not with clothes or books,
but bread, groats, and sugar.
I know the openings in the Wall.
The cats have taught me.
I show Mira on a map her friend Arik has drawn.
"Every crack will be filled with food," Mira says,
bringing our thin soup to simmer on the ring.
I ask to smuggle the bread
through the spot near Krasinski Square
where Michal lives on the other side of the Wall.
Mira knows the danger,
But she nods.
I fall back onto the mattress
and the big room dances with light.

THE BALLROOM OF HEAVEN

Paul Lake *graduated from Towson University in 1975 and went on to become a Stegner Fellow at Stanford, where he received his M.A. He has taught English and Creative Writing at Santa Clara University and Arkansas Tech. Since 2006, he has been the poetry editor of* First Things. *His poems and essays have been widely published, and he has authored two previous poetry collections,* Another Kind of Travel *and* Walking Backward, *as well as two novels,* Among the Immortals *and* Cry Wolf: A Political Fable.

As a Boy Scout, Dad decoded
The *dit-dit-dahs* of Morse, the swashed flags
Of semaphore, bugled "Taps."
At war's end, trumpeted jazz,
Sported a dashing Errol Flynn mustache,
Drove a Mercury coupe, led a brass swing band.

Growing gray, he bought a Mustang,
Captained boats down the Chesapeake,
Tracked game, and bow-hunted bear
In the snow-packed Appalachians.

A snappy salesman with the gift of gab,
He spoke loquaciously, and loved to boast
Of his singular prowess—how he closed a sale,
Bagged a buck, or sang a tenor solo.
Rising late, he rode his route,
Carrying customers' cash, lugged
A black debit book, big as the Baltimore directory
Bound in crocodile hide, holstered a Colt
Semiautomatic, and often flashed
The gold badge bestowed by the Sheriff
When he ran the county's Democrats.

Then cause and effect was suddenly
Suspended. He got lost in a crossword
As in a cul-de-sac. Was flummoxed by phones
As if after Babel. His tongue got
All tangled, his words turned to blab.

Now housed in a hospice, he greets his grown children
"Good guy, good guy," misplacing their names.
Seeing the woman he once swept off the dance floor
And the daughter named after the music they made,
He draws blanks—while a bunch of balloons,
Like a gaggle of gossips who gibber behind him,
Distract his attention, till he's almost unglued.

Pliant as clay, he grows softer and kinder,
More rarefied—as if refined by affliction.
As we quietly mourn his premature absence
And mortified pride, our prayers turn to Please,

Let wings take him up now   to the ballroom of heaven
As a brassy young boy   he took up the horn.
Let him trumpet the tunes   that wooed his young wife.
Make melody again.   Dance the jitterbug of joy.

COMMUTER
& OTHER POEMS

Trey Palmisano is a Rose A. Winder scholar in the Jewish Studies graduate program at Towson University. He holds an M.A. in Theology from the Ecumenical Institute of Theology at St. Mary's Seminary & University, and a B.S. in English from Towson University. He has been writing and publishing poetry seriously since 1998 when he was first encouraged by then-TU Department of English chair, Clarinda Harriss. He has since expanded his portfolio beyond poetry, writing for the Baltimore Examiner *and* Sports Illustrated, *among others. His first book on the theology of Dietrich Bonhoeffer is forthcoming from the academic publisher, Wipf & Stock.*

Commuter

895 loops around the
neck of Baltimore
like a hangman's noose,
tightening as it descends
the Harbor Tunnel.

Half a mile in,
the narrowing slope fills
with carbon monoxide,
invisible footprints
of our fast-paced realities.
Traffic at a standstill,
I remember my
grandmother's fear of small places and the
Zyklon-B that brought
her there.

From the death camps of the War,
where she first purchased her
freedom with good looks, how even
now, each wrinkle carries with
it a fear that she might need to sell herself
again—this poor woman of 80 years
unable to let go.

But necessity has carved out
this path for me,
as it has for so many others
whose lives flicker over highways.

Light smolders at the other end.
I am struggling to make sense of my own escape,
a comfortable lie into which I wake,
undone by my age and small spaces.

Rend

> For those elders who handed down the tradition to us
> taught us that in this hour every creature hushes for a
> brief moment to praise the Lord. Stars and trees and
> waters stand still for an instant.
> —*The Apostolic Tradition of Saint Hippolytus of Rome*

But not just creatures and stars
and trees and waters,
it's how my wife ceases snoring
just before midnight, when
a faint hoarseness built in the lungs
long ago reveals a struggle through which
unconscious breathing fights off allergy,
only to pause a moment at rest.

The apnea to which I was gasping,
or how a purple wave of light
ripples blue from the neighbor's
window, asleep beneath her
TV's sad company.

The few cars that
pass through highway asphalt,
and not their swishing irreverence,
but that the headlamps
remain lost in their own light.

Or how I shift my center of gravity to weightless contemplation
on nights like these.
When the reports of such things
come from men rending their
own fears of death, who make
the nights their waking, and
watch over us all, as if,
in the embrace of some far away
dream they never find,
gathering worlds fall from their pockets.

Polyps

Like marine coral,
we gather on the
skeletons of
our dead, and in
them find the
hiding places
for our own deaths,
where the current holds
us pinned against their
backs, whose backs
keep us from making
our own way without
direction,
and losing ourselves
to stronger currents,
we must sometimes
misjudge the undertow
just to break free.

Here in the Bay

She is somebody's Saturday night.
The harbor lights bend incandescence,
Burn orange streetlamps,
thread through open seams
that spread thin buildings wide.

Time ransoms fate
To the cars that round the block
and those that circle back.
Until she finds the closest shadow,
and steps into her own.

She's careful not to wave.
Tonight, he is hairy and short,
whose hands are flecked with age.
Nervous eyes beat cautiously over
streets one thousand miles
in every direction.

He grips a small bible. Inside,
four crisp bills hang like tongues
from soft leather lips.

"How much for your heart?"
A gravelly voice follows his hand
into the pages, 1 John 3:6,
leads her to the side door,
undresses her shame with a smile.

He might be just as damned
as she is saved, but he talks
a good Jesus, compares track marks
the size of stars in constellations;
the same, her last john says,
lie just overhead,
whose light rarely reaches here,
where so much depends upon faith.

Elements of Tragedy

One of the graces of the Northeast:
a tree falling dead over its roots,
slowly burying itself one leaf at a
time.

Not like the grand conflagrations
of the West, where whole hillsides
are slain by thirst, then fire,
paint a wilderness bare, so that
when mixed with the proper palette
red and yellow make brown.

Rains hold rank from one stubborn
cloud to the next,
bushes burn effigy,
but nothing so holy as a prayer
that
calls for safety.

This is how God uses tragedy,
that mountains stage their
grand peripeteia
in billion year sets,
having once been
sea dwellers long before they
made the land we walk.

We too rose from the sea
if only in our minds, and drenched
our own coats with mud, God
holding
back fire for another time.

MOTHER & OTHER POEMS

*Stephen Zerance is a 2009 graduate of Towson University
and a recent M.F.A. graduate of American University. He has
previously appeared or is forthcoming in journals such as*
West Branch, Prairie Schooner, Assaracus, Bloom, Knockout,
Gertrude, Chelsea Station, Gay and Lesbian Review
Worldwide, Glitterwolf Magazine, *and* MiPOesias. *His poetry
has been featured on websites such as Lambda Literary
Association and Split This Rock. He resides in Baltimore,
Maryland.*

Mother

Madonna of material, I snapped
my rosary, made it into a bracelet for you
at Sunday school, sneaked downstairs
to see you lit before inflamed crosses,
my fingers scented with your patchouli-
cassette. I get drunk, Madonna.
So drunk I sneak leftover drinks
from the bar. I lose myself in the mirror
plucking gray hairs, tug at the sag
in my belly. I want to conquer my fear of
heights, Madonna. Of having roaches or the virus
inside my body. I want a cheap twenty-two

year old lover that doesn't speak
English. I want my hair bleach blond.
I want to go to the bar, Mother. I want
a vodka double, Mother, a double vodka
Madonna on the rocks.

"Mother" originally appeared in the Prairie Schooner

Gay Fiction

Those books I devoured
about the abyss of love
through sex where man
ends solo or can't come
to the party where cancer
entertains, candles lit
then snuffed one by one,
the smoke leaves all
at the farewell symphony.
O my Satan, I've never
been so sad that sex
is still fun when sick
with slut in the hour
of nightwalkers. There
you are: a piece in everyone
at a bar named Hell.
I want to die surrounded
by candy, a city
and a pillar in my mouth.
I'll wear a mask, confess
nothing but these words.
These are days to keep
the dead, to cling to
the living desire inside
not to be afraid. Caution
when consuming men:
the symptoms start
with unsteady muscle

control, wild
laughter, convulsion,
awakening in unfamiliar
surroundings unable
to stand. Welcome
to the strange room.

"Gay Fiction" originally appeared in Toe Good Poetry

Honey Bee

Never mind the wasp—
ball it inside a fist
until the temperature
immolates to lethal.

Or the spider—
leave yourself inside
with stinger detached,

death in minutes.
I was standing, knees
bent, hand over hand
on the driver, my eye
on a dandelion head.

I had beheaded a dozen
that day, their faces
littered the back yard.

The swarm came
from the porch,
a black funnel of bees
inhaling grass, then my

eyes, my shirt. At this
moment, I want to lie
out of need for crisis,
to say I was stung,
my throat swelled,
the taste of metal
in my mouth.

"Honeybee" originally appeared in Seltzer Zine

The Twelve Hours of the Night

Tonight you are not the expert of your body.
Become comfortable with separation, your eyes

masked, the desire to live germinating
out of the inexhaustible bloom of your mouth.

Tonight, a serpent cleaves down both veils
of your body efficiently as scarab, faster

than shadow. Below the spoon fed moon,
seven mosquitoes tread on your tongue

weighted with names you must recite, all
unknown. Remember

what you have not done,
what you have not stolen.

You must kneel down in this terrible place.
You must place your flesh into a tabernacle,

embrace snake. Remember
so far back you consume yourself.

The inner work you've done—oblivion.
Opposition is always there, a bird of prey

moving this boat of your life by a feather.
Write this poem when the last hour winds

itself asleep at the threshold of transformation.
Send forth your words. Stand as voice.

Everything out of your mouth is a lie.

"The Twelve Hours of Night" originally appeared in Seltzer Zine

Skintight

My father hands me gifts he bought Christmas Eve:
an extra-large broadcloth and thirty-four waist khakis.

I dress different from the boys at school. My shirts fall
at my navel; my jeans are skintight.
I am to wear the outfit or my clothes will be ripped apart—

the neighbors are talking. No deals, no exceptions.
We are all there: my mother, my sister on the couch, my father
urging, *Put them on. Put them on.*

I strip in the bathroom with my back to the mirror.
The shirt hangs to my knees, the pants slide on buttoned.
My face is hollow. My skin--deaf, as the audience,

the family await me outside, my mother knocking,
Put them on for your father.

When I step out my mother will be silent. My sister—gone.
My father will clap his hands. He will look me in the eye, ask
me:

Do you feel like a man?

"Skintight" originally appeared in Split This Rock

NONFICTION

THE PART PLAYED BY FORT MCHENRY AND "THE STAR SPANGLED BANNER" IN OUR SECOND WAR WITH GREAT BRITAIN

The Honorable **John Charles Linthicum** *graduated from the Maryland State Normal School (now Towson University) in 1886. Linthicum went on to graduate from University of Maryland School of Law in 1890. He served as a member of the Maryland House of Delegates in 1904 and 1905 and the State Senate from 1906 to 1907. Linthicum was elected as a Democrat to the 62nd Congress in 1911 and served for twenty-two years, representing the Fourth District of Maryland. In 1918, Linthicum was the first to introduce a bill to make "The Star Spangled Banner" by Francis Scott Key the National Anthem, which was likely Congressman Linthicum's best-known legislation, although it didn't officially get named so until 1931. As a congressman, Linthicum was known for supporting veterans and veteran organizations, protecting the environment and natural resources, supporting Woodrow Wilson, opposing prohibition, and working to enlarge and improve the port of Baltimore, including restoring the warship* Constellation. *Linthicum was an advocate in preserving the memory of the siege on Fort McHenry, creating a monument and dedicating it to the soldiers and* *sailors of the War of 1812. In the excerpt of the speech to follow, Linthicum makes an impassioned plea to his colleagues to appropriately pay tribute Fort McHenry and the men who defended it by naming "The Star Spangled Banner" as the National Anthem.*

Speech of Hon. J. Chas. Linthicum of Maryland in the House of Representatives August 5, 1912.
[In this speech, Linthicum first praises the history of the battle song and Fort McHenry, then follows with these words.]

...The country needed a national song to give expression to its patriotism. It wanted only the event to produce it and that event was furnished in the attack on Baltimore. This song of Key's aroused the dormant patriotism of the nation for human nature would not withstand its irresistible appeal to the love of country. It lifted the national spirit from the vale of gloom and despair in which it had been floundering to the sunlit heights of confidence and victory. It heralded the dawn of a new day to our Federal Government. In moral value it was worth ten thousand bayonets.

Conclusion

This, Mr. Speaker, is the story of Fort McHenry.

And now the environs of a great and populous city embrace the little fort which once so heroically defied the King's Navy and the royal forces of war. No longer is its position the outpost of the sentinel. It has become a place of sheltered security, nesting close in the bosom of that city with which its past is so intimately associated. Its walls, once a bulwark of defense, and its guns, once a guaranty of protection, have lost their power. Up to within a few weeks ago it still maintained with pathetic chivalry that position it could fill in name only. Time has ruthlessly robbed it of everything except its golden memories. But as long as our Nation lives, as long as noble deeds beget admiration or the love of country moves mankind, "The Star Spangled Banner" will be sung: and few who sing

"Oh! say, can you see by the dawn's early light" will be able to refrain from going back in mental contemplation to the actual scene at Fort McHenry and dwelling upon that brilliant and stirring chapter which the little fort on the Patapsco contributed to the history of our second war with Great Britain.

The committee on Military Affairs in favorably reporting the bill now before this House said:

"It appears that in the present plan of national defense Fort McHenry no longer occupies a position of strategic military value, and that several proposals have been heretofore offered that it be converted to uses foreign to its present character as a military post. After considering this bill and hearing the statements of those representing patriotic organizations interested in the subject this committee is of the opinion that Fort McHenry is so intimately associated with historical events of vital moment in the early history of our country as to endear it in the affections of all Americans that its use for the sentiment which now attaches to it and that its preservation as a Government reservation under the control of the Secretary of War, and its partial use as a museum of historic relics would be absolutely appropriate with respect to this sentiment. The War Department states that the enactment of the measure will not conflict with the interests of that department and that there is no objection to its passage."

I trust this House will pass this bill. I hope that the little fort which has played such an important part in our history may be preserved to us and to the generations that follow, its ground the shrine of patriotic admiration. I believe that in the near future Congress will see fit to do something even better than protecting from base use this historic spot. I want to see erected near the ramparts of the old fort, plainly discernible to the ships that now pass in peaceful and endless array, a beautiful monument to Francis Scott Key and to the defenders of Fort McHenry at the time of the British attack on that fortification.

WHY MY DAUGHTERS WILL BELIEVE IN FAIRIES

Jeanine Cummins is the bestselling author of the memoir A Rip in Heaven *and novels* The Outside Boy *and* The Crooked Branch. *Jeanine was born in Spain but calls Gaithersburg, Maryland her home town. She studied creative writing at Towson University before living in Belfast for several years. In 1997, she moved to New York City, where she spent ten years in the publishing industry. Jeanine's fiction is deeply influenced by Ireland, where both her novels are set. Her stories draw on her Irish and Puerto Rican heritage. Learn more at jeaninecummins.com. This piece was originally published in* Fairie Magazine. *Read more at www.faeriemag.com*

———

Last summer, when my father-in-law came from Ireland to visit, we took my daughters hiking in the Kaaterskill Wild Forest in upstate New York. My older daughter was five at the time, and her curls were as untamed as the forest. She sprang from boulder to boulder like the spriteliest of wood nymphs, collecting memories into her fingertips: on one hand, the spongy fuzz of damp moss, on the other, the warm, soft grip of her grandfather's hand. She was sweaty and pink-cheeked and happy.

"Hey," I told her, "make sure to watch out for fairies. This is fairy land if I've ever seen it."

She bounced on her toes and squealed, "Yes, Mommy! They always live in the tangly woods, right?"

"That's right."

Her grandfather raised an eyebrow at me and shook his head. Then to my daughter, he said, "Never mind fairies. You should be watching out for bears."

She stopped in her tracks and turned to face him. "Granddad," she said critically, "bears aren't real."

Granddad and I both laughed, but my little girl returned her solemn attention to tracking fairies.

I've thought about that exchange so many times since—

the comic innocence of my child's certainty, and how fragile our small ideas of what's real in this world.

My daughter is six now, and she's in first grade. She is exploring a terrain that is far more treacherous than the knobbly roots and slippery rocks of the Wild Forest; she is learning to navigate the new social landscape of authentic friendship. Gone are the days when her uncomplicated attachments were founded on things like funny faces and a mutual love of cheese.

In the kitchen, my daughter sits at the island with two friends, slurping milk from cups that will leave white puddles on our counter. After snacks, they flee from the room like a thundering tornado of arms, legs, and ponytails. I hear them shrieking and thudding around upstairs. They still retain the lucky caul of innocence; they still laugh with their eyes closed and their hearts open. But not for long.

These six-year-olds are sophisticated. They are ambitious and bright and open. Like glimmering nuggets of ore hacked from the earth, they are unaware of their own potency; they will discover it soon enough. These children have a tremendous capacity for wonder, combined with some natural measure of cruelty. Theirs are the first delicate, prickly, funny, sweet, tender, sharp-edged friendships of life. These kids are practicing how to be in the world, who to be in the world.

It begins. A month after that idyllic playdate comes a forgotten birthday invitation, a surge of jealousy on the school bus, a malevolent remark in the cafeteria about someone's skin, hair, family. One little boy doesn't have the words to fight back, so he uses his teeth and his fists instead. My child gathers it all in with her eyes and ears, and then chants it back to me, her voice thick with anxiety. I have to invent words to soothe my daughter's distress. I have to explain why she wasn't invited to her friend's party, when I don't understand it myself.

Already these children have discovered how to puncture each other with the ugliness of dragons. They know that, if they use their claws, there is a hot squish of mortal humanity beneath the skin. It will get worse as they grow older, as they refine their skills and their bruises.

My daughters will both hurt. They will hurt. They must. Alongside joy and triumph, they will experience, and sometimes inflict, tremendous heartache. I would like to plant a thicket of brambles around their hearts to prevent this eventuality, but I know I cannot. After all, they are going to be teenagers one day. Even a warrior mama cannot guard against life. So what can I do? How do I protect and encourage them?

I must arm them with every Good Thing I can find, and I must do it now, while they are young and receptive. I must choose my weapons carefully. My daughters' armories will include beauty and poetry and stories and music and love. I will heap these armors upon them whenever I can, so that joy might sustain them through the inevitable heartaches to come. Last year I took my first grader to the MoMA, and I stared at her, while she stared, open-mouthed, at Van Gogh's Starry Night. In November, my younger daughter and I spent a day at The Cloisters, where we sat holding hands on the cool stone floor of the Fuentidueña Chapel, completely wrapped in music. Even my three-year-old was moved to silence by the soaring beauty of Janet Cardiff's The Forty Part Motet. (No one was more surprised than I was!) Each evening, we burrow beneath my comforter, close enough so I can smell the toothpaste on their breath, while I read their favorite stories and poems to them.

But beauty is not enough. Their arsenals should also contain magic in all its forms: God, faith, forgiveness, empathy. My children will inherit these words. But I want them to know that there are many different vocabularies for the magic of believing. So my husband and I began by choosing Irish names for them, to echo the ancient mythologies of their heritage, names uttered by fairies once.

In my daughters' bedroom, propped against the bottom rail of their pale pink dresser, sits a fairy door that I bought when my oldest was newborn. It was rather plain at first, but I painted it with purple glitter and strung pearls and gems across it. I fastened a burst of flower buds to its doorstep because I wanted it to look inviting. My daughters have seen it every day of their lives and so, they don't often notice it any more. But they know it's there. They know that, if they leave it unlocked, the fairies might trek through it during the night. (Most fairies are nocturnal, they understand.) The visiting fairies might hide little treasures for my girls, or play funny tricks on them, or perch within the curves of their sleeping ears and murmur dreams into their waiting hearts.

So yes, my daughters will command legions of fairies! Because I want them to know that all things are possible in life. I want them to be open to limitless grace, and to know that they cannot predict or define what that grace might look like.

At six, my daughter knows grace. She is intimately familiar with it; she embodies it. She can stand at the foot of Kaaterskill Falls and hear God's voice scattered and amplified through the whispers of unseen fairies she knows are there. When she is sixteen, and twenty-six, and beyond, I want her to hear it still. When she has her first broken heart, when she is frightened, when she first meets trauma with all of its wicked hooks and weapons, I want her armed. To the teeth.

THE WORKS OF AMY SCHUMER

Amy Schumer is a stand-up comedian, actress, producer, and author who graduated from Towson University with a degree in theatre in 2003. She writes and stars in the comedy series Inside Amy Schumer, *which has been airing on Comedy Central since 2013. She has received a Peabody Award and has been nominated for five Primetime Emmy Awards, and her recent film* Trainwreck *has been a runaway success. Although we tried to track her down through her agent and her Twitter account, Amy was too busy being famous and signing ten million dollar book deals to respond to our messages. So we've decided to offer a brief commentary on a few excerpts from her body of work.*

Towson University has produced some fine alumni, but none have been as impactful as Amy Schumer. In 2015 *Time* magazine featured her in its "top 100 most influential people" list, and she won an Emmy—that's a pretty successful year. Amy was successful in her years at Towson, too; she has fond memories of the recruiting process and the intellectual challenges she grappled with during her years as a theatre major. In her own words, "I went to Towson University in Baltimore... I visited and I won a flip cup tournament and that's why I went there. Scholarship. Full ride. Don't remember a day of it." Okay, so Amy may not remember everything—or even where Towson's campus is (hint: Towson)—but the TU community is proud to call her a Tiger. Here we present examples of Amy's intelligence, fortitude, and comedic ingenuity that make us especially proud.

Though Amy Schumer exudes confidence and an air of invincibility now, she was not always so self-assured. The Amy we all know and love—the Amy with a profound belief in herself—was built in Towson out of unfortunate circumstances. She recalls feeling the following after a regrettable hookup:

> *I was looking down at myself [on the bed with her hookup] from the ceiling fan. What happened to this girl? How did she get here? I felt the fan on my skin and I went, "Oh, wait! I am this girl! We got to get me out of here!" I became my own fairy godmother. I waited until the last perfect note floated out, and escaped from under him and out the door. I never heard from Matt again, but felt only grateful for being introduced to my new self, a girl who got her value from within her.*

This moment, remembered from her freshman year at TU, marked the first step in a journey that led Amy to unprecedented success. Amy has demonstrated this belief in herself consistently; she turned down a 1 million dollar book deal, for example, because she believed she was worth more. Turns out she was right—Simon & Schuster publishing is paying Amy somewhere in the range of 8 to 10 million dollars to write an autobiographical book of essays (the working title being *The Girl with the Lower Back Tattoo*).

Her previous writing has been very successful: she wrote the script for the movie *Trainwreck* herself, and then acted the main part. The semi-autobiographical film features Amy Townsend (The last name, you may discern, is a popular mispronunciation of "Towson.") and details unfortunate hookups and family issues.

Amy Townsend struggles with male acceptance until she meets a sports doctor, Aaron Conners (played by Bill Hader). Aaron insists that they date (Amy was reticent because of commitment issues, but his kindness helped her reconsider), and then helps shape her view of romantic relationships in a more healthy way. The following exchange happens after a minor fight between the two.

AMY: I'm tired; I want to go to sleep—you can go to your apartment. It's nicer than mine.

AARON: No, look—my parents had a saying: don't go to bed angry. We're angry; let's resolve this.

AMY: Your parents weren't that happy.

AARON: They're very happy!

AMY: All right, you wanna talk about it? Wanna get into it?

AARON: Yes!

AMY: Let's get into all of it, right now! Let's do it.

AARON: Yes, please!

AMY: I'll start: you go down on me too much!

AARON: What?

AMY: Yeah, it's selfish! No it is actually selfish! Because you act—don't look like I'm crazy—you act like it's for me, when really it's just to show how great you are. Like you're always helping people.

AARON: So I shouldn't go down on you so much?

AMY: Don't spin this as a way to go down on me so much—that's ridiculous! Of course I want you to go down on me that much!

AARON: So take it down a notch?

AMY: No keep going down on—forget this whole part of the argument, okay? Forget that.

Though Amy doesn't demonstrate the ability to fight productively in *Trainwreck*, she still demonstrates confidence and belief in herself—she's going to be assertive, damnit, and her boyfriend isn't going to take control of the conversation. This scene reveals, quite possibly, insight in to how the new Amy Schumer functions: she may not know what she's doing in all situations, but she has the confidence to try different techniques out until she figures it out.

EXTRA INNINGS

Patrick Smith *graduated from Towson State University in 1990. After starting his career in newspapers, he served as a press aide and speechwriter to several elected officials. After 12 years in the Baltimore-D.C. nonprofit sector, Smith works for the Johns Hopkins University School of Medicine, where he writes about science, research, and medical breakthroughs for various publications. The editor of bugsandcranks.com, a web site dedicated to humor and baseball writing, Smith lives in Baltimore with his wife and a houseful of animals and catcher's equipment.*

When Deborah's mother was dying in a hospice and we had only to wait through her last days, Deb and I sat on either side of her mom's bed and watched the Orioles sweep an early-season weekend series against Kansas City.

The team looked good. The last win of the four-game set launched Baltimore over the .500 mark. They hit for power, they delivered in the clutch, the starting pitchers went deep into games.

Deb's mother was awake during those late spring days. I brought breakfast from a bagel shop and she drank orange juice from one of those bendy straws. We left the tall windows of her room open and a soft breeze blew in, carrying away the morphine-heavy hospice air. Deb's dad would stay all day, showing up at dawn to guard his wife from death. By the evenings, each parent was exhausted from another daylong tangle of never quite saying goodbye to each other, never acknowledging the end, shuffling all around the inevitable.

He'd wait until Deb and I arrived after work, then he'd say his goodnights and drive home alone.

I put the ball game on the television in the hospice room, with the sound barely audible. While the Orioles took care of business against Kansas City, the three of us chatted about how nice everyone was at the hospice.

Deb's mom would fall into a light sleep in the early innings. Each night, Deb and I watched the game while her mom dozed off, talking to each other across the deathbed, sharing workday anecdotes. We made grocery lists and talked about things like oil changes, as if we thought sheer routine would keep her mom alive.

Then the Orioles lost two of three in Tampa Bay. Deb's mom's condition declined. She slept almost all the time. She no longer wanted to drink juice from the bendy straws. The games in Tampa Bay were as quiet as the hospice room. On television, the dome in St. Petersburg looked dark and empty. The Orioles were out of sorts. And when their closer gave up a three-run homer in the second game of the series, it felt like a little piece of life disappeared over the fence with the home run ball.

The Orioles lost again the next night in Tampa Bay, but with much less drama. After a promising first inning, the O's couldn't muster another run all night. They lost 6-3.

The hospice people worked hard to keep Deb's mom comfortable. A combination of illness and medicine made her unconscious. We talked to her, told her we loved her, told her it was OK to go.

Finally, Baltimore got swept in Cleveland and my wife's mother died.

Don't misunderstand me. I don't tie the outcomes of a handful of ballgames to the end of a beautiful life and the devastating loss of a parent. I understand that Deb's mom wouldn't have lived any longer had the Orioles found a hot streak. But for me, the rhythms of the game never felt closer to the rhythms of life.

The results of those Oriole games against the Royals, the Devil Rays and the Indians weren't important. What was important was that the games were played. The Orioles were the only thing that made sense. Win or lose, those ordinary games had a narcotic cadence. Each night during the most difficult of times, they rocked us to sleep. They provided a structure to evenings that otherwise would've been spent staring terrified at a dying mother.

Baseball teaches us to heal and to look to the future. When you're down today, tomorrow will be brighter. By the time the funeral came around, the Orioles were on the West Coast, where they split six games with Oakland and Seattle.

PERMISSIONS AND SOURCES

The River of Dancing Gods, chapter 1, by Jack L. Chalker © Del Rey (1986).

"State Farm" by Dave Housley reprinted with Author's permission.

"My Life as a Mermaid" by Jen Grow from *My Life as a Mermaid* © 2015 used by permission of Dzanc Books.

"The Housewarming" by Ron Malfi, © Ron Malfi, used by permission of the author.

Excerpt from *The Tide King* © 2013 by Jen Michalski used by permission of Black Lawrence Press.

Chapter one of *Newport* by Jill Morrow reprinted with permission from Harper Collins.

"2100" originally published in *Gigantic Sequins*, a literary arts journal, is republished here with direct permission from the author.

"Baltimore" by Kurt Rheinheimer reprinted with author's permission.

Mayhem by Jamie Shaw. Copyright © 2015 by Jamie Shaw. Courtesy of Harper Collins Publishers.

From *THE CATS IN KRASINSKI SQUARE* by Karen Hesse.
Copyright © 2004 by Karen Hesse. Reprinted by permission of Scholastic Inc.

"The Ballroom of Heaven" by Paul Lake reprinted with author's permission.

"Commuter" (Originally published in *Genre: An International Journal of Literature and the Arts*, Vol 23, 2003)

"Rend" (Originally published in *Poems & Plays*, number 13, 2006)

"Polyps" (Originally published in *Hawai'i Pacific Review*, Vol 17, 2003)

"Here in the Bay" (Originally published in *Roanoke Review*, Vol 31, 2006)

"Elements of Tragedy" (Originally published in *National Catholic Reporter*, October 27, 2006) All works reprinted with author's permission.

"Madonna," "Gay Fiction," "Honey Bee," "The Twelve Hours of Night," and " Skintight" by Stephen Zerance, © Stephen Zerance, used by permission of the author.

"Why my Daughters will Believe in Fairies", originally published in *Faerie Magazine* (www.faeriemag.com). Permission given by Author, Jeanine Cummins and Editor of *Faerie Magazine*, Carolyn Turgeon.

From Extra Innings by Patrick Smith. Copyright 2007, McFarland and Company Publishers. Reprinted with Author's permission.

AUTHOR INDEX

PATAPSCO VALLEY PRESS

Patapsco Valley Press is a charitable publisher run by students in Towson University's Master's in Professional Writing Program. Its mission is to facilitate community involvement and service learning among the graduate students in the Professional Writing program. Patapsco Valley Press also publishes fundraiser projects and works for or about local charities, nonprofits, or educational and academic organizations.

26335434R00118

Made in the USA
Middletown, DE
25 November 2015